I0820801

HEALING LEADERS

HEALING LEADERS

7 Steps to Recovery of Self

RAJ SISODIA
AND NILIMA BHAT

Berrett-Koehler
PUBLISHERS

Berrett-Koehler Publishers, Inc.
1333 Broadway, Suite P100
Oakland, CA 94612-1921
(510) 817-2277
bkconnection.com

Ordering Information
Quantity sales. Special discounts are available on quantity purchases by corporations, associations, and others. For details, please go to bkconnection.com to see our bulk discounts or contact bookorders@bkpub.com for more information.
Textbook exam/desk copies. Please consult the General FAQ at bkconnection.com.
Bookstore orders for trade or textbook use. For print books, please contact Penguin Random House Publisher Services at customerservice@penguinrandomhouse.com. For ebooks, contact your favorite distributor.

Distributed to the US trade and internationally by Penguin Random House Publisher Services.

The authorized representative in the EU for product safety and compliance is EU Compliance Partner, Pärnu mnt. 139b-14, 11317 Tallinn, Estonia, www.eucompliancepartner.com, +372 5368 65 02.

Printed in the United States of America

Berrett-Koehler books are printed on long-lasting acid-free paper. When it is available, we choose paper that has been manufactured by environmentally responsible processes. These may include using trees grown in sustainable forests, incorporating recycled paper, minimizing chlorine in bleaching, or recycling the energy produced at the paper mill.

Library of Congress Cataloging-in-Publication Data
Names: Sisodia, Rajendra author | Bhat, Nilima author
Title: Healing leaders : 7 steps to recovery of self / Raj Sisodia and Nilima Bhat.
Description: First edition. | Oakland, CA : Berrett-Koehler Publishers, Inc., [2026] | Includes bibliographical references and index.
Identifiers: LCCN 2025027307 (print) | LCCN 2025027308 (ebook) | ISBN 9798890571496 hardcover | ISBN 9798890571502 pdf | ISBN 9798890571519 epub
Subjects: LCSH: Leadership | Self-actualization (Psychology)
Classification: LCC HD57.7 .S5587 2026 (print) | LCC HD57.7 (ebook)
LC record available at https://lccn.loc.gov/2025027307
LC ebook record available at https://lccn.loc.gov/2025027308

First Edition
34 33 32 31 30 29 28 27 26 25 10 9 8 7 6 5 4 3 2 1

Book production: Happenstance Type-O-Rama
Cover design: Ashley Ingram

To the legacy of the great healing leaders: Abraham Lincoln, Mahatma Gandhi, Martin Luther King Jr., Nelson Mandela, Jimmy Carter, and Pope Francis. May their light continue to illuminate our path and inspire generations to come.

—RAJ SISODIA

To The Mother and Sri Aurobindo.

—NILIMA BHAT

CONTENTS

FOREWORD

BY LYNNE TWIST

When I first met Raj Sisodia, I didn't realize I was meeting someone who would become one of the most meaningful teachers and mentors in my life. We were fellow speakers at a pioneering investment conference—an early, brave attempt to bring new values into the world of business and capital. Long before the term "impact investing" had taken hold, there we were: two voices resonating with the same message, from different but harmonizing roots. My book, *The Soul of Money*, and his, *Firms of Endearment*, carried similar messages about money and life. I remember being deeply moved—stunned, really—by Raj's talk. He quoted the Awakening the Dreamer Symposium, something very dear to my heart, and I thought, "This man *gets it*."

That moment marked the beginning of a friendship, a collaboration, and a soul-level alignment that has endured through years of evolution—in our work, in ourselves, and in the movements we serve.

Raj has always stood for the kind of business that uplifts the human spirit. As cofounder of Conscious Capitalism, a business philosophy that emphasizes a holistic and ethical approach to capitalism, he has called for a more sacred view of commerce—one rooted in love, purpose, and deep care for people and the environment.

Raj was blessed to partner with another brilliant figure in the Conscious Leadership movement, Nilima Bhat, in writing the 2016 book *Shakti Leadership*. That work helped catalyze a global conversation around the need for a more balanced leadership model—one that honors both feminine and masculine qualities in individuals of all genders. Nilima, who bridges the spiritual and the secular, integrates East and West, and is herself a healer, imbues this new book with deep clarity, uncommon vision, and bountiful heart.

Healing Leaders: 7 Steps to Recovery of Self is a brave, tender, rigorous offering from two highly evolved beings who have walked every step they write about. These seven steps—Know Your Self, Love Your Self, Be Your Self, Choose Your Self, Express Your Self, Complete Your Self, Heal Yourself—are not theoretical. They are lived. They are earned.

When Raj told me in 2018 that he was writing a book called *The Healing Organization*, I invited him: "Please come to the Amazon rainforest with me, where I work with Indigenous people." I knew that if he was going to write a book about healing, he would need to seek his own. And to his credit—his deep courage—he said yes. That journey, into the forest and into himself, became a turning point for him. In his encounter with the wisdom of Indigenous shamans and a plant medicine ceremony, he faced the unresolved, softened into the sacred, and emerged healed and even more whole. I witnessed it. I walked with him. And I saw the teacher in him deepen.

Businesspeople often have an allergy to personal development—they see it as something outside the domain of commerce, where success is defined by profit alone. Raj and Nilima recognize that a great leader is one who is committed to developing themselves so they can be of greater service—to their own company and the world.

In a realm where leadership often demands invulnerability, Raj and Nilima invite us to see that our humanity is not a sideline to leadership—it *is* leadership. They fearlessly share their own vulnerability and offer it as a map for every leader willing to turn inward and then lead outward from a place of profound integrity. In addition to their own experiences, they share stories from a dozen or more conscious, heart-based leaders, as well as practices to cultivate such values as presence, authenticity, and self-expression.

Healing Leaders is an extraordinarily rich source of psychological, spiritual, and practical wisdom. Whether you're a CEO, a teacher, a healer, or someone simply trying to live a more conscious life, this book will speak to you. It will challenge you. It will hold you. And if you let it, it will change you.

Read this book. Then read it again. It will not only guide you—it will *heal* you.

Lynne Twist is a global visionary and proactivist committed to creating a future that is environmentally sustainable, spiritually fulfilling, and socially just. She is the cofounder of the Pachamama Alliance, founder of the Soul of Money Institute, and author of *The Soul of Money* and *Living a Committed Life*. Her website is *soulofmoney.org*.

PREFACE

Thank you for picking up this book. For Raj and me, this work represents the culmination and distillation of everything we have explored—both individually and together—over the past two decades. It is more than a book; it is a *manual for life*, a guide to recovery for the wounded leader in you and in each of us.

When I completed my first two books, *My Cancer Is Me: The Journey from Illness to Wholeness* and *Shakti Leadership: Embracing Feminine and Masculine Power in Business*, I knew that a third book would be necessary—one that would weave together the Integral Healing journey of the first with the Conscious Leadership journey of the second. Those books summarized my two decades of work both as an Integral Yoga practitioner and cancer coach and as a Gender and Conscious Leadership consultant and trainer.

In my work with cancer patients, I encountered a concept that deeply resonated with me: the *wounded healer*. It describes a healer—whatever their role—who has endured the same wounds as those they seek to help. The most powerful wounded healers are those who have done the work to heal themselves. Even if they are not fully healed, they have traveled far enough along the path to guide others with wisdom and compassion.

What is fascinating is that healing is never a one-way process. Every therapeutic encounter—whether between doctor and patient, coach and leader, or others—has the potential to transform both people involved.

After a decade of coaching cancer patients, I shifted my focus more fully to working with business leaders, founders, and organizations committed to conscious business and Shakti Leadership. What

I observed was revealing: Even the finest, most committed leaders inevitably hit a wall. Their early success stalled. Despite their best efforts, nothing seemed to work anymore.

When I put on my *healer* hat instead of my *coach* hat, I began to see a pattern: The very same healing principles that helped my cancer patients move forward could also help these leaders break through their blocks and rise to a higher level of impact.

That is because, at their core, leaders—*even conscious leaders*—are human beings first. And like all human beings, they carry wounds—traumas from childhood, setbacks in their personal or professional lives—that linger in the psyche. Yet traditional management training rarely reaches deep enough to surface and heal these wounds. True leadership transformation requires an inner journey, a psycho-spiritual approach. If we are to lead others with clarity and purpose, we must first learn to lead ourselves from within.

I remember saying to Raj, after seeing so many conscious leaders struggle with being stuck, "We need therapy for leaders."

This book is our answer to that call.

Raj and I are both wounded healers and wounded leaders—two sincere humans on our own conscious leadership paths, striving to be changemakers for a better world. In these pages, we offer the elixirs and insights from our own *heroic journeys*—the lessons that have helped us heal and grow so that we may better fulfill our purpose: the *Conscious Capitalism* movement for Raj and *Shakti Leadership* for me.

As Raj often says, "Hurt people hurt people." But the opposite is also true: Healed people heal people. Healed leaders heal leaders—and their organizations.

Raj's book *The Healing Organization* explored how companies can be forces for healing in the world. This book takes that journey inward: It is a seven-step program for healing *yourself* as a leader so that you, in turn, can become a force for healing in the lives of those you lead.

We *can* do good and do well—not just as businesses, but as human beings.

That is our hope and blessing for you, dear reader.

—*Nilima Bhat*

I would like to add my welcome to this journey.

Healing Leaders is a call to rediscover the essence of leadership in our time—an essence grounded in self-awareness, compassion, and the courage to lead from the heart. This book is born from decades of research, practice, and conversations with leaders around the world who have embraced their role not just as stewards of performance, but also of the human spirit.

In these pages, you will find a pathway back to your truest self: a journey of knowing, loving, and choosing yourself, of healing what has been wounded and claiming what has always been whole. These seven steps to recovery of self are not just a route to more effective leadership; they are a blueprint for a life that is aligned, authentic, and deeply connected to a higher purpose.

May *Healing Leaders* offer you inspiration, challenge, and hope. May it help you become the leader you are called to be—a healing presence in a world that needs it more than ever.

—Raj Sisodia

CHAPTER 1

The Journey Ahead

The longest journey you will ever take is
the journey from your head to your heart.
—SIOUX PROVERB

In a world beset by complex challenges, where crises often seem relentless, many of us are feeling the toll. Rising anxiety, depression, addiction, and even suicide rates reveal a collective struggle to find inner peace, joy, and purpose. As the world grows more chaotic, so too does the need for personal healing and alignment.

This book is designed to be your guide on the journey to greater self-awareness, deeper healing, and more conscious leadership. It distills timeless wisdom, powerful contemporary insights, and proven practical steps into a clear, actionable framework that yields powerful, tangible shifts in awareness and actions. Drawing on real-life experiences and the accumulated wisdom of ages, it offers a straightforward, step-by-step approach to align who you are with what you do and how you relate to others. The result? A transformation that empowers you to bring your fullest, most balanced self to every aspect of your life.

This journey should ideally be completed over six months, with each of the seven steps unfolding in phases of two to three weeks. By thoughtfully completing each exercise and fully engaging with the principles and practices described here, you will deepen your sense of well-being, personal fulfillment, and peace of mind. You will experience transformations not only in how you feel but how you lead, and your relationships—at work, with family, and in your communities—will benefit as you bring your best self to each encounter.

The commitment you made by opening this book is vital. You are, after all, your own most important stakeholder—more than your children, your parents, or your partner. Your primary responsibility is to yourself: to nurture and grow your whole being into the most potent and healed version of yourself, allowing you to experience the deepest life satisfaction and to create the most positive impact in the world.

Our choices have the power to create joy or suffering, for ourselves and for all the lives we touch. This is especially true for those who lead. Leaders have a profound impact on their organizations, influencing whether they become forces of healing or harm in the world. When leaders elevate themselves, they elevate the lived experience of everyone around them.

What we share in this book is the result of years of dedicated personal practice and careful curation of tools and methodologies from the world's greatest wisdom and wellness traditions. These insights and practices are not just theories; they are proven pathways toward wholeness and healing.

This book focuses on the inner life, because it's this inner transformation that enables us to positively impact the world at large and the lives of those we love and lead. To paraphrase Rudolf Steiner, "We can do nothing more helpful for the world's further evolution than to evolve ourselves."

THE "self" VERSUS THE "SELF"

In this book, we'll be exploring the concept of the "self," a term that invites a distinction between the "small self"—our individual selves—and the "larger Self," which represents both the collective consciousness and our own Higher Self.

Any path to personal growth and lasting transformation inevitably requires evolving our spiritual intelligence. We must acquire the wisdom to connect our small self—our egoic personality, limited by time and space—with the higher aspect of ourselves, the larger Self that transcends the boundaries of our individual identity and connects us with all life and the universe itself.

Many mystics have described connecting to the larger Self as an experience of profound unity. They may be walking through a forest or watching a sunset when suddenly they feel their personal identity dissolve. In these moments, they describe a sense of oneness: *I am the sap running in that tree. I am the wave in the ocean. There is no separation between me and that.* This experience of unity is a glimpse into our true, limitless nature that is intertwined with all existence.

The journey you are undertaking through this book is about integrating the two selves: knowing and honoring the small self while simultaneously expanding into the boundless, interconnected Self.

We are each both unique and universal—distinct individuals and inseparable aspects of a greater Oneness. Our small self, with its particular story and gifts, plays a vital role in expressing the unique facets of the Whole that we embody.

We have labeled the steps in this journey in a deliberate way, distinguishing between "your Self" and "yourself." The difference lies in the nuance of meaning and the context in which each term is used, especially when discussing self-awareness or personal growth. When separated into two words, "your Self" refers to the core essence or true being of a person, the authentic, inner nature that transcends everyday roles or labels. On the other hand, "yourself" is your everyday self, the small self that most of us are able to understand and are in touch with. This is the self we will mainly be working with in this book.

This distinction is not always possible to capture perfectly in language. For the sake of simplicity, in the chapters that follow, we will generally refer simply to "yourself." We suggest that you hold these two concepts of "self" in your mind as you read; it will then become natural and easy for you to understand how we intend the term at any given time. Should this become confusing, just stay with whatever feels simpler for you to align your thinking with.

THE STEPS

Healing Leaders is structured around seven simple yet profound steps on the journey to creating a life of significance, purpose, and joy:

1. Know Your Self
2. Love Your Self
3. Be Your Self
4. Choose Your Self
5. Express Your Self
6. Complete Your Self
7. Heal Yourself

All of these steps require your small self to work with your larger Self. The seventh step is titled "Heal Yourself" because it is the small self that must be healed and integrated into the wholeness of the larger Self. The larger Self is already whole; it does not need healing.

As Figure 1 illustrates, this is not a one-time journey but a cycle that can be repeated at various points in one's life.

These steps first manifested in Raj's consciousness during a four-day silent retreat in 2018 at Peace Village Learning and Retreat Center in Upstate New York. We see them as a direct download from our collective consciousness. In our minds, that accentuates the power of these steps as being, in a sense, divinely ordained—a transmission from the source, not the product of individual authorship. The following is a brief introduction to what each step entails, to prepare you for the journey ahead.

Know Your Self

The journey of self-discovery begins with knowing yourself.

It is surprising—and sobering—how many people go through life as strangers to themselves. Knowing yourself is the foundation upon which everything else rests. Who are you, at your deepest core? What is your true nature, beyond the labels you have acquired and the roles you play? What are the qualities that define you, the values

FIGURE 1. The Seven Steps to Recovery of Self

that guide you, the passions that bring you alive? These questions may seem simple, but they take us to the heart of our existence.

This is not a one-off process of discovery but an ongoing, ever-deepening exploration. It requires committing yourself to a life of awareness, inquiry, growth, and self-honoring. It enables you to evolve in alignment with the deepest truth of who you are. In knowing yourself, you come to understand that you are both a singular being and an integral part of something much greater than yourself. This awareness brings a profound sense of meaning, connection, and peace.

Love Your Self

Knowing yourself is essential, but it is only the beginning. The next step is to reach a place of truly loving yourself—not just tolerating, accepting, or learning to live with who you are, but embracing yourself with genuine warmth, compassion, and affection. Loving yourself means appreciating the whole of your being, including your strengths and your limitations, your light and your shadow. It's about seeing yourself as worthy, not for what you achieve or how well you conform to others' expectations, but simply because you are you.

Through this journey, you will come to know that loving yourself is the foundation for being able to receive the love of others and give love to others. Self-love, grounded in self-acceptance and self-compassion, is the most empowering gift you can give yourself, transforming not only your relationship with yourself but also your capacity to connect with the world around you.

Be Your Self

Once you come to truly know and accept and love yourself, the next step is to fully be yourself. This means feeling at home in your own skin, grounded in a profound sense of inner peace. Being yourself requires shedding the layers of conditioning, fear, and self-doubt that may have kept you from expressing your true essence. It's about moving beyond the need for approval or validation from others and instead resting comfortably in your own presence.

In choosing to be yourself, you make a powerful declaration: "I am enough, just as I am." This declaration liberates you, giving you the courage to pursue your unique path and contribute your gifts to the world. Being yourself means honoring your inner voice and letting it guide you, rather than being swayed by societal expectations or the fleeting opinions of others.

Choose Your Self

Choosing yourself is an act of profound self-liberation. It means embracing your past and your present—the journey that brought you here—and actively creating your future. It is a radical decision to step out of the role of victim, no longer allowing past experiences to determine your self-worth or sense of possibility. Instead, it's about saying, "I choose everything that ever happened to me, even the hardest experiences. I wouldn't wish them upon anyone else, but they have shaped me into the person I am today and directed me toward my life purpose."

Choosing your life means embracing all of it—the joy and the suffering, the mistakes and the triumphs, the people who lifted you up and those who let you down. It's saying, "Even if I had the opportunity to choose again, I would still choose my family, my background, and every one of my experiences." This is not about dismissing the pain or denying any injustices you may have faced. It's about honoring those moments for the wisdom they brought and the resilience they cultivated in you.

Express Your Self

To fully manifest your destiny and your potential, you must express your unique gifts to the world. This is about choosing growth over comfort, stepping into the unknown, and showing up with courage. It means embracing your individuality and sharing your essence, your ideas, and your talents, rather than staying silent or "fitting in." Expressing yourself calls you to live consciously, not compulsively, making intentional choices rather than following the crowd or surrendering to habit.

Most importantly, expressing yourself is about discovering and living your purpose, pursuing your passions and harnessing your gifts in a way that meets the needs of the world. It points you toward a life path that is both meaningful and fulfilling.

Complete Your Self

To complete yourself is to become whole. It is a journey toward integrating four primary energies we each carry within ourselves: the masculine, the feminine, the elder, and the child. Many of us go through life as only partial expressions of our four-fold selves—quarter or half human beings, rather than complete human beings.

To become whole is to honor and harmonize all aspects of ourselves, embracing the full spectrum of our humanness.

The goal is to become what Nilima calls the "Wise Fool of Tough Love." This archetype represents the integration of all four energies: the wisdom and maturity of the elder, the innocence and joy of the child, the strength and courage of the masculine, and the compassion and nurturing of the feminine. The Wise Fool of Tough Love embodies the ability to approach life's complexities with both depth and humor, to navigate challenges with both strength and tenderness. It's about cultivating a heart that loves wisely and a mind that opens with curiosity (and a gut that guides you with strength!). When you complete yourself, you are no longer bound by a single mode of being or constrained by old patterns and roles.

Heal Yourself

The final step on this journey—healing yourself—is perhaps the most profound and challenging one for many of us. We all carry wounds and traumas; this is part of the universal human experience. Yet most of us go through life unaware of, or unwilling to acknowledge, the extent of our own pain. We think, "I didn't serve in a war, I haven't experienced extreme suffering," and so we dismiss our scars. But the truth is, life itself brings hardship, and we each carry our own dose of post-traumatic stress and emotional injury. Until we recognize and begin to address these wounds, we remain vulnerable to suffering and prone to causing suffering in others. Unhealed pain within us makes us reactive. We don't understand why we feel and act as we do, driven by forces buried within us that shape our words and actions in unconscious ways.

True healing transforms us. As we heal, we soften, become more empathetic, and learn to approach ourselves and others with patience and kindness. The more we heal, the more our past loses its hold over us, and we become free to live authentically and respond thoughtfully rather than reactively. Healing ourselves empowers us to move from victimhood to empowerment, fear to love, and isolation to connection.

This process of healing will never be complete, but each step we take lightens the load we carry. It is not only a gift to us but to everyone we encounter. It is one of the most courageous and meaningful journeys we can undertake.

THERAPY FOR LEADERS: HEALING BEFORE LEADING

For years, Nilima has felt a deep need for a book titled *Therapy for Leaders*. In many ways, this is that book. Too many leaders are charged with vision yet held back by unhealed wounds. Consciously or not, they carry their unresolved issues into the realm of leadership. No amount of external training can create a whole, healed leader. This requires inner healing, delving into one's psychological landscape and addressing the effects of past traumas.

Until you work on healing yourself, you'll remain stuck. We've seen leaders build remarkable organizations, even inspire global movements, and then hit a wall—an invisible but profound barrier that halts their growth and may even cause them to regress. It's not a matter of insufficient skills or resources; it's a matter of unhealed soul wounds. Left untreated, these wounds prevent leaders from pushing beyond this hidden threshold.

As a holistic health coach, Nilima views leadership from the perspective that every time a leader regresses or falters, they are being pulled back to an old wound—a place within that is crying out for attention and healing. To unlock the energy trapped in those hidden scars is to release oneself for the next level of growth. Therapy for leaders is not an option; it's essential if they are to have a positive impact in moving humanity forward.

Many psycho-spiritual traditions recognize two vital tracks: spiritual growth and therapeutic healing. If we skip the therapy, we risk what's known as "spiritual bypassing"—a tempting detour into a world of idealism, where "all is love" and "everything is perfect." But this bypassing neglects the essential foundation of psychological wholeness. It fails to tend to the wounded child within. Every unhealed trauma remains a silent buried landmine, waiting to be triggered.

The psyche knows. Like an ocean tirelessly sending wreckage back to the shore, it brings forth what we've tried to ignore and bury.

Painful memories, unhealed wounds, suppressed fears—these all rise from the subconscious, asking to be cleansed, healed, embraced. The ocean of our inner world insists we tend to our wreckage; only then will the tides carry us forward.

This book, and the seven-step program within it, takes leaders on a therapeutic journey—a journey to connect to their true selves, heal the roots of their pain, and emerge as leaders who are not just skillful but also whole, so they can experience freedom and fulfillment in their life and their leadership.

As you embark on this journey, we strongly urge you to integrate two practices into your life: silence and meditation. These will make a profound difference in how deeply you are able to explore and integrate the lessons of each of the steps.

HEALING LEADERS PRACTICE
Twenty-Four Hours of Silence

The quieter you become,
the more you are able to hear.
—Rumi

Our world is filled with constant distractions. We are rarely disconnected from the incessant flow of information and stimuli that hijack our attention and prevent us from connecting to our higher selves, to the inner guidance that is always available to us but gets drowned out by all the external noise.

One of the most powerful experiences you can have is to make space for an extended period of silence in your life. Many highly influential people do this. Take Yuval Harari, one of the leading intellectuals of our times and author of the global bestsellers *Sapiens, Homo Deux* and *21 Lessons for the 21st Century*. Yuval meditates for two hours every day and goes on a sixty-day silent retreat in India once a year. He credits these practices for the powerful insights he is able to bring to his writing.

While we are not recommending anything so intense, we invite you to experience the magic of silence in your own life. Identify a

twenty-four-hour period when you can be completely disconnected from all external stimuli: your cell phone, email, social media, newspapers, TV, as well as social interactions with others (including your partner). Try to spend as many hours as possible in nature. Keep a pen and a journal with you, and nothing else. Use the journal only to record any profound insights you receive during that time.

Remember, silence also means no nonverbal communication with the outside world: no written notes or gestures.

HEALING LEADERS PRACTICE
Mindfulness Meditation

Mindfulness meditation is a gentle yet powerful practice of learning to be fully present in the moment, letting go of worries about the past and future. It helps calm the mind, eases stress, and fosters a deep sense of well-being and connection.

To begin, find a quiet space where you can sit comfortably, on either a cushion or a chair. Gently close your eyes or soften your gaze. Take a moment to check in with yourself, noticing any tension or restlessness, and set an intention to practice with kindness and patience.

Focus your attention on your breath. Feel the air moving in and out of your nostrils and notice how your belly rises and falls with each breath. Let your breath be natural, without trying to control it.

When thoughts, emotions, or distractions arise (and they will), simply acknowledge them without judgment. Gently bring your attention back to the sensations of breathing. Each time you do this, you're strengthening your ability to stay centered and present. Start by performing this exercise for five minutes, and gradually increase the length of your meditations over time.

Mindfulness meditation isn't about "emptying the mind" or achieving a particular state. It's about being present with whatever is happening—pleasant or unpleasant—without clinging or pushing away.

As you practice, you may begin to notice subtle shifts: feeling less reactive, more patient and accepting of yourself and others, and more able to

navigate life's ups and downs with calm and clarity. The key is consistency and a spirit of gentle curiosity.

Above all, remember to relax and enjoy the journey. With time and regular practice, mindfulness meditation can be a nourishing way to reconnect with yourself and the world around you.

SEEDING INTENTION FOR THE JOURNEY AHEAD

Before you begin this journey, take a moment to connect deeply with yourself and clarify your intention for this experience—what you hope to gain from reading and living the principles of this book. When you set a clear intention and align your whole being with it, you pave the way for growth and transformation.

Keep a pen and a journal nearby. After the following guided visualization, record what you receive.

To begin, sit with both feet on the floor and straighten your spine. Squeeze and release your muscles to relax them. Shake out your limbs and let go of all tension. Take a deep breath, then exhale slowly. Rest your hands comfortably on your thighs. Softly close your eyes or leave them half-closed, creating an inner focus free from outside distractions.

As you settle, allow your breathing to deepen and your body to relax. With each breath, your mind calms and your heart opens, connecting you to your Higher Self.

Envision yourself at the end of this journey, having completed the book and each of its exercises. Experience the satisfaction of knowing that you showed up fully, dedicated the necessary time and energy, and reaped the benefits of this commitment. In this moment, with clarity and calm, remember why you embarked on this journey. Sense your deepest desire—what you hoped to receive and take away from this experience. Let yourself feel joy that this intention has come to fruition.

Now, hold a sense of gratitude in your heart for the gift of this experience. When you're ready, pick up your pen and record what you are feeling in your journal. Begin with, "Dear Higher Self, I am deeply grateful that my intention has been fulfilled." Let the words flow from your heart, capturing the essence of what you intended and what you received from this journey. Write in the language of your soul, continuing to breathe deeply as you express yourself.

When you finish, gently place your pen down. Read over your words, absorbing them fully. Let each word settle in your being as if you were tasting the most delicious fruit. Savor this feeling of fulfillment and allow it to permeate every cell of your body. Let a gentle smile of gratitude and joy form on your face.

Finally, release this intention to Life's greatest intelligence. Let go of any attachment, any clinging, any need to control the outcome. Trust that it will manifest in its own time and way, through the wisdom of your Higher Self. Breathe, let go, and feel free.

Now, let's begin the journey.

CHAPTER 2

Know Your Self

Knowing yourself is the beginning of all wisdom.

—ARISTOTLE

The first step to recovery of self is to know yourself. This is the foundation of all that follows. You know the basics: how you identify yourself internally and to others, where you come from, the traditions you carry. But what does it mean to truly *know* yourself, beyond the labels of career, name, birthplace, religion, education? And why is this important?

To know yourself is to dive beneath the surface of your identity, to reach into the depths of your inner world and understand the unique rhythms of your thoughts, the passions that make your heart race and the strengths that are yours alone. It is about discovering your raw, unfiltered essence, who you are at your core.

The journey to self-knowledge involves deep reflection on two vital elements: your nature and your identity. In Sanskrit, the term *svabhāva*, derived from *sva* (self) and *bhāva* (being or becoming), describes the intrinsic nature or essential disposition of a person or entity. Your *nature* is the essence you were born with—the purest version of you, unaltered by outside influences. Your *identity*, on the other hand, is the accumulation of roles, labels, and beliefs that life experiences and societal expectations have layered upon you.

In this chapter, we will guide you through exploring both: the innate qualities that define you and the identity you've crafted along the way. The knowledge you gain will form a powerful foundation for achieving fulfillment, moving forward with clarity, and living a life that is not only meaningful but also profoundly joyful.

IDENTIFY YOUR INNATE QUALITIES

From our earliest moments, we spend years—even decades—learning about the external world. Yet few of us are taught to explore our inner world. As Sharmadá Foundation founder Patrick Connor says, "We are living in a twenty-room mansion, but most of our us spend our lives in the lobby." To know yourself is to understand your own beauty, dignity, and worth. This requires connecting with your true nature, recognizing what you value, and identifying the passions that drive you. Self-knowledge starts with understanding your essential qualities—those that define you at your core, distinct from the roles you play or the expectations you strive to meet.

The journey of self-discovery begins with questions like: Who am I, really? What defines me? What makes me come alive? These questions uncover the values and traits that are fundamental to your identity. As children, we receive a steady stream of messages about who we should be, based on external factors such as family background, culture, gender, and even birth order. These labels can mask our true essence. We must look beneath them to discover who we truly are.

None of us fashion ourselves from scratch; we are shaped by unseen forces, molded in ways we don't understand. Raj's mother sensed something that defined him from an early age, nicknaming him "Pappu," a term meaning innocent and pure-hearted. She, too, was a gentle soul, simple and kind. That name accurately captured essential elements of his nature: trusting, peace-loving, idealistic.

Raj writes:

The qualities I was born with contrasted starkly with the culture I was born into: the warrior caste in India, steeped in patriarchy, hyper-masculinity, and feudal power. My grandfather held a hereditary title and owned vast lands, managing generations of laborers under a system that bore haunting resemblances to indentured servitude. It was a world of inherited privilege, aggression, pride, and the relentless suppression of women and workers. I was raised amid constant conflict, in an atmosphere of dominance and harshness.

Within me was a quiet, opposing force. My mother's soft presence filled my early years, as my father was absent until I was seven. She nurtured my natural inclination toward peace and harmony—perhaps too much. As I grew, I became conditioned to avoid conflict at all costs, becoming, in a way, the "chief harmony officer" of my own life.

My father saw my qualities as flaws. To him, my innocence was weakness; my idealism was naivety; my trust was foolishness. I absorbed his judgments and began to see myself through his critical lens. For years, my father's voice became my own inner voice, reminding me of all the ways I fell short.

Under the sway of my worldly, ambitious, hyper-masculine father, I rejected my "Pappu-ness" for decades. I came to hate that nickname. "Don't call me Pappu," I'd insist. "My name is Raj." To be called Pappu felt like being branded a fool and a simpleton. I wanted to be shrewd, ambitious, and powerful like my father.

For much of my life, I struggled with these questions: Was I Raj, the ambitious, worldly one? Was I Pappu, the innocent one? Was I the dutiful son of a Rajput family? Was I Indian, American, an engineer, a professor, a writer? I grappled with many identities, each adding a layer of confusion.

There is great power and relief in embracing our true nature. When we reclaim what's inherently ours, we find strength that is both gentle and profound. Accepting and embracing my inner "Pappu" has allowed me to live in harmony with myself, and to see that kindness, trust, and a peace-loving nature are not weaknesses; they are the greatest strengths I possess. At the same time, I recognize that aspects of "Raj"—such as ambition and boldness—are also core to my nature.

HEALING LEADERS PRACTICE
Take Your Inventory

Take a moment to look inward and reflect on your unique qualities. In your journal:

1. **Make a list of your natural gifts and talents—qualities that have always been a part of who you are.**
2. **On another page, list your well-developed skills—the abilities you've honed through effort and experience.**
3. **Finally, note your core values—the beliefs for which you would take significant risks or make major sacrifices.**

Which of your qualities have you dismissed or doubted?
How can you reclaim them?

WHAT IS YOUR IDENTITY?

The question "Who am I?" seeks to uncover not just our innate traits and core values, but also the many dimensions that shape our identity. Identity is a *psycho-social construct*: a combination of our sense of self (self-concept and self-esteem) and the social and cultural factors that influence how we are perceived by others.

Often, our greatest conflicts—personal, societal, or global—are rooted in the question of identity. Who do we see ourselves as? Who do others believe us to be? The tension between these frequently competing visions fuels much struggle, pain, and division. Yet these are questions we cannot avoid. To live fully, we must understand and embrace our identity, shaping it in a way that resonates with others without losing our own sense of self.

To begin, we must step back and conduct an honest "identity review." To support this process, we've created a Personal Identity Review worksheet (Figure 2). Many of the questions are binary choices that ask, for instance: Are you Eastern or Western? Modern or traditional? Some descriptors, such as religion and nationality, are open-ended. Perhaps caste doesn't define you, but class might: Do you see yourself as part of the lower, middle, or upper class? For some, these labels are crucial; for others, they're inconsequential. But they all play a part in defining our identity.

OBJECTIVE: To help clarify the descriptors that define your identity

DIRECTIONS:

1. In the list below, tick the item in each pair that you identify most with. Try to make a choice for each, even if it's difficult (some may not apply, such as Father/Mother and Brother/Sister; you can leave these blank). There are no right or wrong answers.
2. Don't overthink it. Choose quickly. BE TRUE TO YOURSELF!
3. Fill in the blanks at the bottom as well.

☐ Eastern	☐ Western	☐ Feminine	☐ Masculine	☐ Son	☐ Daughter
☐ Northern	☐ Southern	☐ Old	☐ Young	☐ Parent	☐ Child
☐ Cultured	☐ Natural	☐ Fit	☐ Unfit	☐ Colonizer	☐ Colonized
☐ Modern	☐ Traditional	☐ Fair	☐ Dark	☐ Capitalist	☐ Socialist
☐ Arts	☐ Science	☐ Short	☐ Tall	☐ Optimist	☐ Pessimist
☐ Creative	☐ Logical	☐ Local	☐ Foreigner	☐ Introvert	☐ Extrovert
☐ Rational	☐ Emotional	☐ Rich	☐ Poor	☐ Aggressive	☐ Submissive
☐ Thoughtful	☐ Spontaneous	☐ Educated	☐ Uneducated	☐ Focused	☐ Easygoing
☐ Player	☐ Spectator	☐ Well-traveled	☐ Untraveled	☐ Dreamer	☐ Practical
☐ Father	☐ Mother	☐ Big-town	☐ Small-town	☐ White	☐ Other
☐ Believer	☐ Non-believer	☐ Salaried	☐ Entrepreneur	☐ Spiritual	☐ Material
☐ Conservative	☐ Liberal	☐ Brother	☐ Sister	☐ Religious	☐ Secular

Religion ____________________ Race ____________________

Nationality ____________________ Profession ____________________

Caste ____________________ Generation ____________________

Sexual Orientation ____________________ Class ____________________

Gender Identity ____________________

FIGURE 2. Personal Identity Review

Some labels may seem unimportant at first glance—such as skin tone (fair or dark)—but turn out to carry deep significance. In Indian culture, for instance, light skin is prized, especially in the "marriage market." Nilima remembers how her sister was dubbed the "pretty one" because of her lighter skin, while she was reassured with "Oh, you're the smart one."

Adds Nilima:

> *Being brown-skinned wasn't something I thought about, but it impacted my life profoundly. I'll never forget being an eight-year-old in Germany, playing in a sandbox when a White boy, who I'd thought was my friend, suddenly sneered, "Go away, you Brown girl." In that moment, I became aware of my color as a marker that disadvantaged me.*

Our identity often reflects our deepest values. The qualities and labels we hold onto reveal what we cherish most, becoming symbols of who we are. Identity is both inherited and chosen. Some aspects, like gender or nationality, are given to us by nature and society, shaping our sense of self before we even have a choice. As we grow, we also adopt identities of our own making. We might claim ourselves as global citizens, choosing to transcend the borders and roles assigned to us.

In our modern world, identity has grown increasingly complex. One critical binary for self-reflection is that of *colonizer* and *colonized*. For generations, colonized peoples endured occupation, war, and subjugation. Many became disconnected from their indigenous roots, unaware of the cultural riches buried under layers of colonial influence. The effects of colonization are enduring; they seep into our minds and systems, shaping academic frameworks, social hierarchies, and legal structures. Today, we live in an era of gradual "decolonization," where societies and individuals are working to heal these legacies.

In India, for example, there has been a powerful resurgence of cultural pride, with many people seeking to reclaim "Indic knowledge systems" and the ancient wisdom lost during British rule and the reigns of other invaders, such as the Mughals. Some passionately reject the remnants of colonial influence, striving to re-root themselves in their heritage. Others—especially the urban educated and Western-oriented—still gravitate toward Anglo-European systems and values. This divide has profound effects on national identity, effectively creating two Indias: one that embraces the colonial name "India," and another that insists on the original name "Bharat."

Nilima, like many Indians raised in a liberal, urban setting, grew up looking to the West for guidance and inspiration, embracing a worldview aligned with the colonizer's. Now, she feels drawn to her roots, finding a sense of pride in the wisdom of Indic traditions, but without rejecting the West outright. Instead, she strives for balance and integration—a blend of ancient and modern, indigenous and universal.

Nilima's journey of self-discovery also taught her the significance of her identity as a woman. Growing up, she was very much her father's daughter, almost dismissing her mother's influence: He was a powerful figure who commanded attention, and she faded into the background in comparison. Only later did she come to recognize and value her mother's feminine versions of strength, resilience, and quiet power.

Nilima shares:

I feel very fortunate to have had an almost idyllic childhood with two very committed and loving parents. My dad was an upright Indian Naval officer from small-town Orissa who joined the Navy because his widowed father could not afford his college books. The Indian Navy shaped his innate academic strengths into excellence and made him a skilled engineer, who went on to build an oil tanker in Germany called Shakti *(for those who know my work, this word became integral to my life's trajectory).*

From my dad, I learned and deeply internalized the three "H" values he had seen his own father live by: honesty, hard work, and helpfulness. Each of these was accompanied by a poignant story about Bappa, as he called my grandfather. He never tired of telling these three stories, even though he lost most of his memory after a near-fatal road accident at age fifty-seven. That accident forced him to retire from active work life, after which he turned to spirituality before eventually passing on beautifully at the ripe age of eighty-nine. His thirty-two-year struggle with a disabled body and mind—endured with extraordinary grit and courage—and the way he died full of gratitude for life, always striving to become a better person, have been a profound lesson for the family he left behind.

I came to truly "see" my mother as I watched her fully step into her role as his primary caregiver, embodying formidable feminine qualities: endurance, selfless care, and self-sacrifice—often to the point of self-neglect. She was the perfect complement to my father: creative, enthusiastic, ambitious, and quick to forgive. (The three Fs—forgive and forget and have fun—gracefully sum up what she has modeled for me.) She made life something to look forward to. My core identity as a woman and a human being was shaped largely by the best I aspired to inherit from her—traits I had consciously rejected for many years—and completed by the best I wished to carry forward from my father.

HEALING LEADERS PRACTICE
Who Am I?

Identify the three core descriptors from the previous exercise that resonate most closely with who you are—the unshakable "I am this." Then, list five additional descriptors that are important, even if secondary. Finally, list five descriptors that, while not primary to you, impact your life in significant ways. Arrange them in three circles, each containing the previous one, as shown in Figure 3. If the descriptors in the earlier worksheet don't capture your essence, add your own—for example, Nilima's top three identities are that she is a woman, a global Indian, and a conscious changemaker.

Take your time with this exercise; it will offer a lens for understanding your place in the world. The goal is to discover core aspects of yourself that you may never have fully acknowledged.

As you work through this exercise, pay attention to your reactions and insights. Reflect on the following:

Top three **How does each of these descriptors shape the essence of who you are?**

Next five **These descriptors may represent areas for growth, a guide for becoming your truest self.**

Last five How do these descriptors impact your life? What might you need to navigate more mindfully?

A participant in our workshop shared: "My top three felt close to my soul—things I cherish deeply. The last five surprised me, bringing up traits and experiences I rarely think about but which have shaped me in difficult ways. It's not easy to accept, but I can see how they impact how I show up in the world."

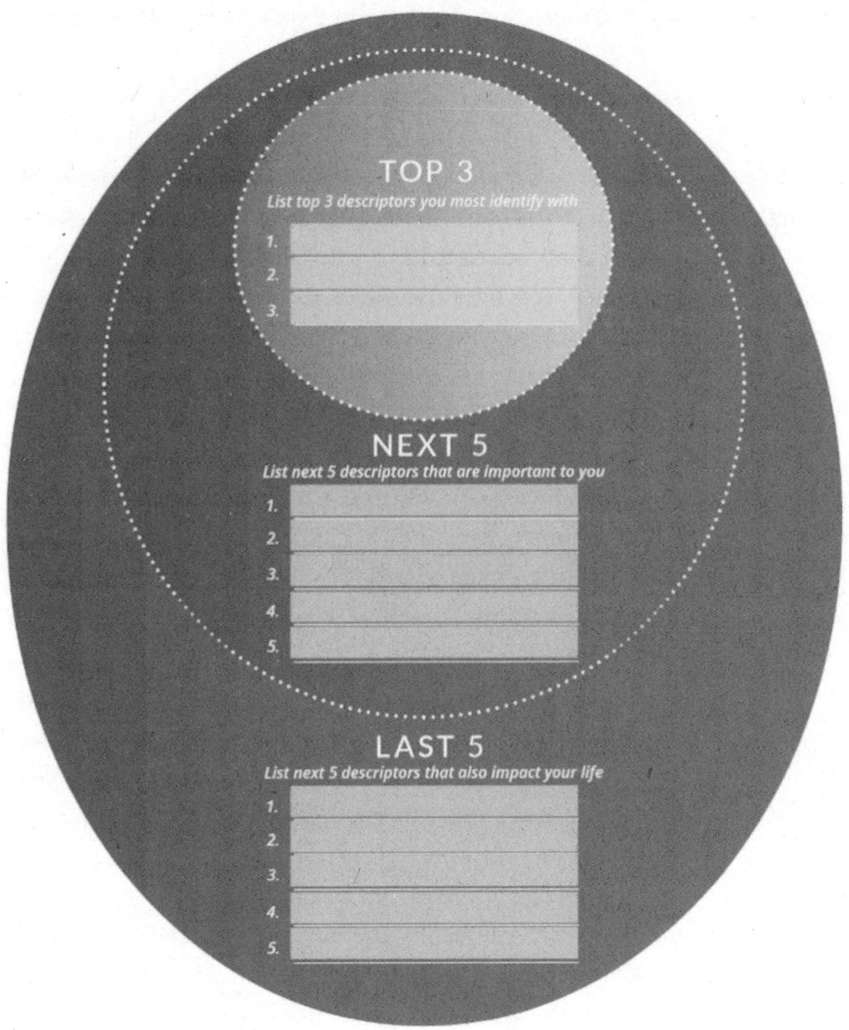

FIGURE 3. Who Am I?

Race, for example, is a factor many of us take for granted. If you come from a privileged racial background, you might not realize the immense influence of race on the opportunities available to you, how others perceive you, and your sense of belonging. But for those from marginalized backgrounds, it is often a defining aspect of their reality.

Our identity is our personal anchor, our foundation for understanding and interacting with the world. By identifying our key descriptors, honoring them, and sometimes challenging them, we move closer to an identity that is expansive, inclusive, and true. Embrace this journey, for the deeper you go, the richer and more meaningful your experience of life becomes.

BEING SEEN FOR WHO YOU ARE

Find a friend you trust to share in this reflection, or explore it privately through journaling. Begin by considering your top three identity descriptors—those qualities that feel central to who you are. Where did these parts of you come from? How have they shaped your life? While they may empower you, they also come with a cost: When you choose one identity, you may reject its opposite. What do these descriptors add to your life, and what doors do they close?

Think about what triggers these aspects of your identity. What are your flashpoints—moments when you feel a surge of defensiveness or passion? Nilima, for instance, describes herself as deeply identified with her Indian heritage: "When someone criticizes India, I get triggered, even if I might agree with their point. Somehow, I feel that I have the right to criticize my country, but they don't."

Write down what typically sets you off. If you're working with a partner, ask them to hold space for you: to listen without offering solutions or judgment. When you finish, they can acknowledge your vulnerability by saying, "[Your Name], I see you." This simple phrase carries profound weight. When we reveal something so essential to our being, our core self seeks validation, not through approval but through recognition as truth.

Opening up in this way—revealing the parts of yourself you usually guard—requires a vulnerability we rarely display. In everyday interactions, we tend to avoid these deeper connections; we keep things light, exchanging small talk and maintaining emotional distance. Imagine how different things would be if we introduced ourselves not with our titles, but our truths.

In this spirit, Nilima encourages us to bring depth into our introductions: "I can no longer make small talk at social events, chatting about inconsequential things with people I may never see again. My soul withdraws. Now I ask questions like, 'What shaped you?' 'What are some of the peak experiences in your life?' 'What excites you most today?' We become closer to ourselves and each other through these meaningful exchanges." Consider how much richer you might feel after such interactions, inviting others into a dialogue that immediately creates trust, vulnerability, and connection.

Nilima shares her personal approach to dialogue:

> *In a deeply psychosomatic sense, our physical heart is the gateway to our true Self. I used to swing between emotional highs and lows in dialogue—sometimes caught in the heady high of spiritual bypassing, revealing only my most polished, "best self" to the other, only to find the dynamic eventually plunging into a swampy low, where fears and judgments surfaced on both sides.*
>
> *Over time, I made a conscious commitment to stay anchored in my "non-dual" heart space—that place we call Presence. I learned to soften the hard breastplate of defense, allowing myself to move into a tender, heart-broken-open place. When I resist my ego's panic—the fear of being hurt or having my vulnerability used against me—I often find that something shifts. The other person responds to my openness and begins to feel safe enough to drop their guard as well.*
>
> *The masks fall away. We both leave the conversation not only fulfilled, but touched by a sense of the sacred that entered the space—an elevation into mutual respect for our shared humanity, regardless of whether we agreed or disagreed on the topic at hand.*

ROLES AND IDENTITY: THE TAPESTRY OF SELF

Consider the connection between the roles you play in life and the identity you carry. What roles—such as parent, partner, leader—profoundly define who you are? Is it a strength or a vulnerability to let our roles define us?

Roles are complex; they can be empowering, grounding us with purpose and meaning, but they can also limit us if we cling to them as absolute truths. As you embark on the journey of self-discovery, hold onto this question: Do my roles reveal my true self, or do they conceal it?

Exploring your identity is like tracing the rings of a tree outward. Your three core descriptors are only the beginning. The next layers—the middle and outer descriptors—provide a deeper, more nuanced view of who you are and what has shaped your sense of self. As you reach the outermost layer—the roles and experiences that have impacted your life in some way—you begin to see that every label, every role, is open to interpretation.

Take the concept of "believer." What does it mean to identify as one? For Nilima, the answer is expansive. "Anyone who knows me knows that I'm a big believer," she says. "I love God across all religions, all cultures—God, Goddess, whatever name we give the Divine." Yet recently, she faced a challenge to this identity when her son, a young adult who had attended esteemed universities in the United Kingdom and later Yale University, came out as an atheist. She recalls her surprise: "He never discussed it with me, and then one day I read it in his blog. Here I am, a proud believer, and my child is an atheist. How could this be? This isn't just about differing beliefs—it's about the identity we each carry, and how we navigate these differences. have to acknowledge and respect his autonomy and choices." Here, Nilima touches on a universal truth: Identity is not static, and the identities of those closest to us can influence and shape our own—perhaps even pushing us in the opposing direction.

This journey is not about choosing *either/or* but finding the space for *both/and*. Polarity thinking—holding seemingly opposing ideas in harmony—is an essential tool for self-understanding. Our minds are accustomed to binary thinking, which often leads to inner and outer conflict. Life's richness lies in embracing paradox, in understanding that we can be both believer and skeptic, compassionate and strong, unique and a part of something greater.

Identity and Leadership

The relationship between identity and leadership is profound. Conscious Capitalism, a philosophy centered on purpose-driven business, champions *conscious leadership*—a way of leading that goes beyond traditional theories of authority. Former Whole Foods co-CEO Walter Robb says it simply: "The leader you are is the person you are." If you don't know who you are, you cannot lead with authenticity and strength. Self-awareness isn't optional for conscious leaders; it's a necessity.

Your leadership reflects the way you hold your identity. If you carry it unconsciously, it will show up as a blind spot, leading you into obstacles you won't understand. But if you carry it consciously, you can navigate life and leadership with clarity, using the aspects of your identity as tools rather than letting them weigh you down. Knowing who you are as a person empowers you as a leader, enabling you to engage authentically with those around you and to embrace the challenges and responsibilities leadership brings.

In his influential book *Authentic Leadership* and subsequent works, former Medtronic CEO Bill George argues that true leaders are defined not by their titles or power but by their ability to remain true to their values and lead with empathy and conviction. He highlights the importance of leaders developing a deep understanding of themselves, embracing their unique life stories, and being transparent in their interactions. This fosters trust and creates strong, values-based organizational cultures.

The Wisdom of "Being Nobody"

Identity provides a stable sense of self, a unique place from which we relate to the world. At the same time, it acts as a filter, shaping and sometimes distorting the world we see. This distortion can be subtle, yet it profoundly affects how we interact with others, revealing unconscious biases within us.

Imagine stripping away these layers, these labels that you've accepted as your identity. What would reality look like without the filters of nationality, religion, or social status separating the people you encounter into "like me" and "not like me"? If you remove those filters, you meet others simply as human beings, free from the assumptions that typically color our interactions. This perspective invites curiosity instead of judgment, unity instead of division.

At our core, we are all worthy, valuable, and whole. Yet we often spend years shaping our identities to gain external approval, forgetting that our true worth lies in simply being. The spiritual teacher Ram Dass often spoke about the radical freedom of "being a nobody." His teaching invites us to question the need to "be somebody"—to build an identity that is impressive or validated by others. This relentless pursuit of "somebody-ness" traps us in the confines of ego and disconnects us from the vast interconnectedness of life. Being "nobody" isn't about insignificance; it's about liberation. It's a way of moving beyond the narrow, self-centered narrative and stepping into our boundless, compassionate essence. Only when we let go of the need to protect or project our identity do we truly become free to love, serve, and connect with authenticity.

Similarly, the Indian mystic Sadhguru teaches that the attachment to a rigid sense of self prevents us from experiencing the fullness of life. Our identities are often shaped by internalized cultural and familial influences. He suggests that by loosening our grip on these identities, we can experience life with greater ease and joy, stepping into a natural state of being that is limitless and peaceful. When we stop clinging to our labels, we can embrace a more expansive reality, in which we are connected to all things.

UNDERSTAND YOUR PRIVILEGE QUOTIENT

Each layer of our identity reveals something essential about who we are in the world. On a personal level, do you identify as a man, a woman, or nonbinary? What does that identity carry with it in terms of privilege or limitation?

Family is the next layer: What is your racial background? What religion were you raised in? From there, we move outward into the broader context of society. Are you part of a particular social class or caste? This can affect the opportunities you have, your sense of security, and the way you're perceived by others.

We then expand to nationality: Are you from a developed nation or a country in the Global South? This geographical marker alone often determines access to resources, opportunity, and privilege. Finally, on a planetary scale, we all identify as human beings—entities that hold dominion over other species and exert profound influence on the Earth's ecosystems. Figure 4 illustrates these different layers.

A line runs through all of them, marking the boundary between privilege and lack of privilege. Your "privilege quotient" is the sum of these identity markers—a concept that highlights significant inequalities in our world. For instance, being a man often confers more privilege than being a woman. In many parts of the world, being White or Christian carries more privilege than being a member of another race or religion. Those born into higher social classes or castes typically enjoy privileges unknown to those in lower classes. If you're from the Global North, you likely experience advantages that those in the Global South may only dream of. As humans, we collectively hold a privileged position, wielding unchecked influence over other species—often at the expense of the planet's health and balance.

Two people standing side by side may look similar but carry vastly different privilege quotients. Life is not a level playing field; when we apply for a job or attempt to seize some other opportunity, the scales are rarely balanced. Identity is profoundly entangled

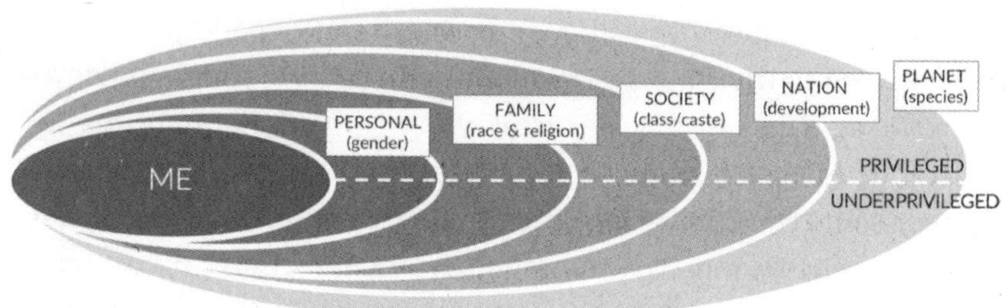

FIGURE 4. Identity and Privilege

with power. If this link did not exist—if there were no "privileged" and "underprivileged" markers attached to our labels—we would simply be uniquely different, without the accompanying historical and societal empowerment or disempowerment.

Hold Identity and Privilege Lightly

Understanding your privilege quotient isn't about dismissing your identity or denying its significance. It's about seeing it clearly, recognizing the privileges and limitations it carries, and choosing to hold it lightly.

Our identity provides a useful anchor, a means of navigating the world—but if we grip it too tightly, it can become a barrier to our growth and evolution. When we hold it lightly, on the other hand, it becomes a doorway rather than a wall—a bridge to our deeper self, a means of connecting with others and honoring our shared humanity. Instead of being confined by who we think we are, we open ourselves to others' realities, recognizing their identities as equally valid, equally cherished. In making space for others to be seen as they are—without categorizing, judging, or diminishing—we step into a place of mutual respect and understanding that allows for a deeper connection.

In recent years, the power of identity to unite has been overshadowed by its potential to divide. Identity politics has intensified, transforming political and cultural labels into polarizing forces. In the United States, for example, political identities have driven a wedge between many friends and family members. People identify so closely with their political beliefs that they forget their shared humanity. What were once differences of perspective—Democrat or Republican, lower taxes or a stronger safety net—have become high-stakes battlegrounds, where one's political stance is viewed as defining their entire character. This "us versus them" mentality fractures societies. And the problem isn't unique to the United States; countries like India, Brazil, Mexico, the United Kingdom, Israel, Hungary, and Poland are experiencing similar divisions. As history shows, this polarization can threaten a nation's cohesion at its core.

Learning to hold our identities lightly is a way to counter this. Embrace the roles and labels that help define you, but let them remain flexible, allowing for growth, complexity, and empathy. This shift allows us to act from a place of conscious power, as whole, interconnected beings who are not limited by labels. This is where true strength lies: in honoring both our unique selves and our shared humanity. The journey of identity is thus both an inner and an outer one: a quest to see clearly the privileges and limitations we have inherited, to claim our power consciously, and to free ourselves from the constructs that hold us back. Only then can we step into the fullness of who we are, empowered to live, love, and lead in a way that uplifts both ourselves and the world around us.

Beyond Privilege: The Power of Soul Force

While layers of privilege are often real and consequential, history offers powerful examples of individuals who transcended these constraints. Leaders like Gandhi, an Indian man from the merchant caste, and Mother Teresa, a woman in a world favoring men, found their strength not in societal advantage but in what Gandhi called "soul-force"—rather than relying on institutional power, they claimed their moral authority.

These leaders defied the labels that limit others, choosing to rise above any sense of personal disadvantage or powerlessness. By calling out injustice and hypocrisy, they stood firm in the strength of their essence, operating from a power source that transcends identity. This is what we call *Shakti*—an innate, ethical power that originates from the deepest part of the self. When you connect with your Shakti, you are no longer defined by race, gender, class, or privilege. You tap into a truth that is unassailable, a power that has nothing to do with external markers.

When you live in this space, you become profoundly effective because you are no longer playing the conventional game. You move beyond the constructs of privilege and limitation, choosing instead to lead from a place of unshakable integrity and inner strength.

HOW IDENTITY CAN LIMIT YOU

Knowing who you are is essential. It provides the foundation for your sense of self and purpose. But as crucial as identity is, it can also become a cage, restricting growth when clung to too tightly. Our identities should empower us, but they must remain flexible, evolving when they no longer serve us.

Here are five clues that your identity may be holding you back, each one an invitation to release what no longer serves your higher self:

DISPROPORTIONATE REACTIONS

When you react with unusual intensity, your identity may be driving your behavior. For example, if someone makes a passing criticism about your country of origin and you respond with anger or defensiveness, you're likely reacting based on a deeper identity wound. Ask yourself, "Why does this affect me so strongly?" Recognizing that it's your national identity being triggered allows you to step back and choose a calmer, more grounded response. Your true self lies beneath the trigger, waiting for the opportunity to engage with openness rather than defensiveness.

QUICK JUDGMENTS AND FORCEFUL CRITICISM

When identity wields too much control, we often find ourselves judging or criticizing others sharply. These reactions can signal that an aspect of your identity feels threatened. If you find yourself quickly dismissing someone's opinion or feel the need to correct them forcefully, pause and ask, "What in me feels at risk here?" Often, it's your ego identifying too closely with a role or belief. Realizing this frees you to listen and learn, rather than reacting from a place of insecurity.

PERSISTENT NEGATIVE EMOTIONS

Recurring negative emotions, such as stress, fear, resentment, or shame, can indicate that an aspect of your identity is acting as an emotional trap. For example, a woman who feels dismissed or disrespected in a conversation may notice anger or resentment rising within her. By recognizing, "I am identifying as a woman and feeling discounted," she gains awareness that her reaction is rooted in her identity rather than the situation itself. This awareness allows her to respond from her true self. For all of us, regardless of gender, there is power in questioning where labels may limit us and how we can move beyond them.

RESISTANCE TO NEW PERSPECTIVES

Identity can act as a barrier to growth when we cling too tightly to the belief that "This is who I am." When our sense of self feels fixed, we resist new ideas or perspectives that challenge it. Ask yourself, "Am I holding on to a version of myself that no longer fits?" When we allow ourselves to be fluid, we create space for expansion and transformation, embracing new ways of being that are more aligned with our present reality.

FEELING STUCK

When you feel stuck or notice that your usual strengths are no longer effective, it may be a sign that you have outgrown an identity you once relied on. This is often a quiet clue, yet it's a powerful invitation to reflect and ask, "What part of me needs to evolve?" Our strengths should grow with us. When they stop serving us, it may be time to loosen the grip on an old identity and step into a new way of being.

Let these clues be invitations. Each moment of awareness opens the door to greater self-discovery, guiding you to the powerful realization that you are so much more than any one aspect of your identity. Embrace that truth, and allow yourself the freedom to grow, adapt, and evolve in ways that honor the whole of who you are.

HOW IDENTITY EVOLVES

The beautiful truth about identity is that it's not fixed; it's fluid, a living tapestry that is constantly rewoven as we progress through life. Identity is intertwined with the roles we play, the experiences we gather, and the wisdom we accrue. As these elements shift, our sense of self transforms with them, like a river gradually changing course.

The following are some of the powerful forces that shape and reshape our identity:

LIFE STAGES

Identity naturally evolves as we pass through life's chapters: childhood, adolescence, parenthood, elderhood. Each stage brings new relationships, new responsibilities, and a new understanding of self. The role of mother may transform a woman's identity, while the role of grandmother reveals still other aspects of her self. These transitions invite us to explore previously hidden facets of ourselves, allowing our identity to unfold in tandem with life's changing seasons.

TRAUMA

Life-altering experiences—for example, a serious illness like cancer—can leave an indelible mark on our sense of self. Trauma shifts our inner landscape, reshaping how we view the world, our relationships, and our purpose. A survivor of such a transformative ordeal may find that they've stepped into a new self: one that is informed by resilience, a recognition of fragility, and a profound awareness of life's brevity. Along with the pain comes the possibility of growth, offering a new understanding of who we are. While trauma changes us, healing offers the opportunity to integrate those changes and let our identity blossom beyond the scars.

CONTEXT

Who we are often depends on where we are. When we step into a new environment, we are given permission to explore and express different parts of ourselves. A Westerner traveling in India might discover a freer, more spiritual side of themselves. These contextual shifts might seem out of character to friends back home, but they reflect a deeper, authentic expansion of identity. We are not one fixed self; we are many selves, shaped by place, time, and setting.

CHOICE

Most empowering of all, identity can be transformed by conscious choice. The values we embrace, the goals we set, and how we decide to live our lives all shape our identity. You might choose to embrace a healthier lifestyle, follow a new spiritual path, or change your career aspirations, and this might become a central feature of your identity. Identity, when chosen with intention, can become an empowering declaration of our values, shaped not by circumstance but by will.

Embracing the evolution of identity requires openness and curiosity, a willingness to release old versions of ourselves to make way for new ones. Your identity is not a rigid set of characteristics; it's a mosaic, a collection of experiences, roles, choices, and contexts. Each phase, each challenge, each conscious decision adds color and texture to who you are.

When we allow ourselves to evolve, we free ourselves from the past, shedding identities that no longer serve us. Let identity be a fluid companion, a shape-shifter that mirrors your growth, your resilience, and your boundless potential.

IDENTITY IN THE WORKPLACE

Identity is at the center of any meaningful conversation around diversity, equity, inclusion, and belonging (DEIB). Each individual brings to the workplace a unique blend of history, culture, values, and experience. When we understand and honor these differences, we unlock the potential for workplaces to be more than spaces of productivity—they become places of transformation, innovation, and genuine connection.

Identity is the pulse that drives diversity, allowing us to harness the brilliance found in our differences. Distinct perspectives enable fresh ideas and groundbreaking outcomes, breaking free of the predictable. Embracing diversity is a commitment to valuing the kaleidoscope of viewpoints that fuels creativity and drives progress. When each person is truly seen, we open the door to richer possibilities.

Equity is rooted in an awareness of identity, with all its nuances and complexity. When we center this awareness in our pursuit of fairness, we become more attuned to the subtle biases and power dynamics that shape our interactions and opportunities. This clarity enables us not only to acknowledge these imbalances, but to dismantle them. Equity calls for leveling the playing field, creating an environment where every individual has fair access, free from the weight of discrimination and systemic barriers. In doing so, we foster a culture where all voices can be heard.

Inclusion is the active embrace of difference, welcoming diverse thoughts, ideas, and perspectives, and celebrating the richness they bring. It goes beyond merely opening the door to varied identities, instead weaving them the very fabric of the organization. True inclusion is about creating spaces where all voices resonate, where each individual feels not just accepted but truly valued. It's about cultivating an environment where every person can contribute authentically and help shape the path forward.

At the heart of it all is belonging—the deepest expression of identity in the workplace. Belonging is a sense of connection, of being seen and valued. When people feel they belong, it transforms the workplace from a transactional space into a community. Belonging drives engagement, promotes well-being, and inspires loyalty. It turns a job into a calling and colleagues into allies.

To create a workplace rooted in DEIB is to build a culture where every identity is honored, every voice matters, and every individual knows they have a place and a purpose.

Adds Nilima:

> *Diversity of thought and culture often becomes a major challenge when trying to reconcile employee identities after a merger or acquisition—especially between large, well-established brands. I experienced this myself, and even though this happened back in 1997–1998, I still vividly recall the intensity of the internal conflicts.*

At the time, I was head of corporate communications for ESPN STAR Sports, overseeing more than twenty-five countries across the Asia-Pacific region. The organization was a newly formed joint venture between Disney and News Corp, created to put an end to the escalating bidding wars between them for sports broadcasting rights in emerging markets. Financially, the merger made sense. Culturally, however, the divide was stark; the team was split almost evenly between those who came from—and thought like—ESPN, and those from News Corp.

It quickly became clear to me that my "internal PR" role—harmonizing these groups into a new, shared identity—was even more important than my "external PR" role of securing media coverage for the brand. I threw myself into creating fun, meaningful events and initiatives designed to shift the mindset from "us versus them" to "let's play well together" and "let's bring out the best in each other." I thoroughly enjoyed that challenge—turning cultural tension into creative possibility.

CONSCIOUS LEADERS SPEAK
Know Yourself

What does it mean to truly know yourself? For the conscious leaders we interviewed for this book, the journey of self-knowledge is a dynamic, unfolding process—one that invites honesty, humility, and continuous inner listening. Their stories remind us that leadership begins with self-awareness, and that knowing yourself is both the foundation and the fuel for leading with integrity, love, and courage.

Doug Rauch, former president of Trader Joe's and former CEO of Conscious Capitalism Inc., brings a grounded and spiritually informed lens to the question of identity. For him, the journey of knowing oneself is both deeply human and fundamentally divine. "I think knowing yourself is foundational—but we have to ask, which self are we talking about? The deep, divine self—what the wisdom traditions call the *Atman* or the ground of being—is always there, like the sun behind the clouds. But most of us only glimpse it. What we typically come to know is the evolving self in relationship—the one shaped by family, school, community, work. And that's real, too. We discover who we are through how we live, how we respond, how we choose."

Whole Foods Market cofounder John Mackey's spiritual journey began with a radical disintegration of self. At age twenty-two, a powerful psychedelic experience altered the trajectory of his life. "I was an existentialist and atheist at the time—disconnected from purpose, meaning, and any spiritual dimension. But during that LSD experience, my ego dissolved and I became one with everything. I realized that the essence of who I am is eternal—it never began, and it will never end. Not my body, not my personality, but my essential self. That realization changed everything."

Ed Freeman—renowned professor, philosopher, and the father of stakeholder theory—frames self-knowledge as a lifelong philosophical inquiry. His journey began as a teenager distancing himself from the evangelical Christianity of his upbringing, seeking instead to author his own understanding of the world. "Knowing yourself is not a box you check. It's a project that lasts your whole life. You think you understand your values, your past, your aspirations—until life shows you something new. You're always discovering more. For me, it's all part of trying to live an integrated, authentic life. Doing that is anything but simple. You fail. You fall short. But you try again. And that trying—that's the work. It's not a destination; it's a way of being."

Gervase Warner, former CEO of the Caribbean-based Massy Group, experienced a pivotal moment of self-knowledge during a Landmark course that challenged his long-held personal narrative. "I always thought of myself as purpose-driven. But the first real breakthrough came when I had to read aloud the story I'd been telling myself: that I had overcome every obstacle through hard work and determination. They played 'Old MacDonald Had a Farm' in the background as I read. It was disorienting—and enlightening. It made me see: This is just a story. That shook me. I began to realize that what I thought was my truth was, in many ways, a constructed persona. That was the beginning of a deeper knowing—a peeling away of the mask I had created to succeed."

For Simon Cohen, CEO of Henco Logistics, champion swimmer, and judge on *Shark Tank Mexico*, self-knowledge is not a static achievement—it's an ongoing, inner conversation. It evolves with age, shaped by introspection and the changing seasons of life. "Knowing yourself isn't a one-time thing; it is a daily dialogue. Knowing myself at thirty was different from knowing myself at forty. And now, at fifty, I'm discovering another layer. I talk to myself—literally—as a we: the heart, the soul, the mind, and the body. Now I find myself in the third quarter of life, asking: What do we want to do with the twenty-five good years we may have left—if we're lucky to have them? It's not just about what Simon wants anymore—it's about aligning the different parts of myself."

Kip Tindell, cofounder of The Container Store, exemplifies a rare and steady clarity of self. Unlike many whose journey of self-discovery is catalyzed by trauma, Kip's was nurtured by love. His story is a testament that leadership rooted in joy and trust can be as inspiring and transformative as that born from adversity. "I was lucky—I grew up in an environment of unconditional love. That gave me a kind of ballast, a grounded sense of who I was. I didn't have to perform or pretend. I could be fully myself from a young age, and that shaped how I led. I trusted people, and I believed in them. That belief began with how I was raised—and it stayed with me throughout my life."

For Kristin Engvig, founder and CEO of Women's International Networking (WIN) and WINConference, the journey to self-knowledge involved peeling back layers of shyness, sensitivity, and social conditioning to rediscover the wild, joyful self she had been as a child. "I always felt I was 'too much'—too creative, too wild, too free for my mother, who was more domestic and traditional. But I was the child who climbed trees, traveled worlds (metaphorically), danced with abandon. For years I had a voice in my head saying, 'You're too much.' But that wasn't mine. That was conditioning. Knowing myself meant reclaiming that wild girl—and realizing she is me."

Marisa Lazo is the founder of Pastelerías Marisa and a judge on *Shark Tank Mexico*. Getting to know herself has been a lifelong, therapy-supported journey of self-inquiry and self-definition—choosing between multiple roles and shedding layers of cultural conditioning to find the core of who she really is. "I couldn't be a psychotherapist, a baker, and a mom all at once. It took over a year of therapy to realize I was happier building a business—opening stores, creating with people. I chose the path that brought me joy, not just meaning. And ever since, I've continued the work of knowing myself—through therapy, reflection, and simply paying attention to how I feel when I'm being truly me."

Morad Fareed is cofounder of FC Mother and former member of the Palestinian National Football Team. For him, true self-knowledge came through radical identity unlearning—a rejection of résumé-based self-definition in favor of soul presence. "We're told that we are our résumé—our nationality, our job title, our marital status. But all that is reductionist. Who I really am isn't any of that. It's consciousness having an experience. At some point, I started watching my life instead of just living it. I wasn't Morad—I was witnessing Morad. That changed everything. I don't want to shrink into any one thing. Today I'm a birdwatcher, tomorrow a philosopher. I contain multitudes—and I refuse to live in a box."

For Timothy Henry, long-time consultant and now CEO of Conscious Capitalism Inc., learning that he was adopted added layers of complexity to his journey of self-knowledge. Timothy's late-life reconnection with his biological family brought a tectonic shift in his understanding of himself, deepening his sense of identity. "Because I was adopted, I always had this part of my identity that was missing. Finding my birth mother in my late forties was a turning point—it filled in a part of my story I didn't know I was missing. Suddenly, I could see myself in others: the same gestures, the same language. That was a huge shift. For the first time, I felt more comfortable in my own skin. In my adopted family, I never quite fit in—physically, intellectually, or emotionally. When I met my biological siblings—all of whom went to Harvard—I realized just how much of who I am came from biology. But I also had to integrate the adopted experience. I am a hybrid of both."

Self-knowledge is essential not just for personal fulfillment, but also for conscious leadership. Each of these leaders has walked a different path, yet they all share a deep commitment to inner truth. Whether awakened by crisis, catalyzed by therapy, sparked by love, or revealed through stillness, self-knowledge is the compass of conscious leadership. It grounds us not in certainty, but in presence. It takes honesty, curiosity, and the courage to keep asking: *Who am I, really? And how can I live that truth more fully, every day?*

Knowing yourself is the first step on the path to embracing yourself fully. It's the foundation on which we build self-love, acceptance, and compassion. When we understand who we are—our unique strengths, our vulnerabilities, and even our shadows—we lay the groundwork for a more profound, nurturing relationship with ourselves. This brings us to the next step: *loving* yourself.

CHAPTER 3

Love Your Self

Love is the only force capable of
transforming an enemy into a friend.
—MARTIN LUTHER KING JR.

Knowing yourself and *loving* yourself are two distinct journeys. Few people understand this better than Raj. As his self-awareness grew, so did the weight of external judgments. Most painfully, relentless messages that his essential qualities were flaws to be corrected came from his father.

"Don't trust anybody," Raj's father would say, criticizing Raj's natural inclination to see the good in others. When Raj expressed his peace-loving nature and desire for harmony, his father countered, "You need to be rough and tough." His idealistic questions about suffering and social injustices such as India's dowry system were dismissed: "You need to go along to get along." Even his academic excellence, demonstrated by straight As, earned only a cursory glance and the cutting remark, "What really matters is to be 'street smart.'"

Believing these messages, Raj began living in a way that conflicted with his authentic self. He buried his idealism beneath cynicism, hid his trusting nature behind guarded suspicion, and forced himself into confrontations that felt foreign to his soul. For decades—from his pre-teen years into his fifties—he lived largely as someone else's version of himself.

Loving yourself means cherishing the qualities that make you unique, seeing them as gifts rather than flaws. Many of us obsess over our "shortcomings" (which may be strengths in disguise) yet rarely take time to appreciate our strengths. Real self-love requires acknowledging and embracing these, whatever they may be.

At some point we must consciously choose to honor our unique, innate traits, embracing them as powerful gifts rather than flaws to hide. If we reject a desire for harmony, we invite conflict; if we deny our trusting nature, we become suspicious. Innocence is a universal birthright, often lost over time as we grow cynical or strategic. But we can choose to return to it—not as naivety, but as a principled way of being that avoids causing harm and is rooted in mutual respect and goodwill.

"Denying your true nature is certainly not a formula for happiness," Raj reflects now. "It took me a very long time to accept who I am. But when I finally embraced these qualities—my idealism, my trust in others, my desire for harmony—I realized they weren't weaknesses at all. They were the source of my true power in the world and the engines for me to be able to do the work that I was born to do."

Raj's experience illuminates a crucial truth: Knowing yourself is only the first step. The greater challenge lies in learning to love what you find—especially when the world tells you to be someone else. True fulfillment doesn't come from molding yourself to others' expectations, but from embracing and celebrating your authentic nature.

This chapter will guide you on the journey from self-knowledge to self-love, from rejection to acceptance to celebration of who you truly are.

AN EPIDEMIC OF SELF-LOATHING

In today's world, self-loathing has reached epidemic proportions. Many people are trapped in cycles of self-hatred, failing to offer themselves the love and compassion they might give to others—even strangers. Bruce Lipton, author of *Biology of Belief*, estimates that 80 to 90 percent of people struggle to love themselves.

Ancient wisdom underscores the need for self-love. The Buddha's teachings remind us, "You yourself, as much as anybody in the entire universe, deserve your love and affection." Yet, for many of us, this truth remains distant and difficult to embrace. While we are quick to offer kindness to friends and acquaintances, we struggle to extend the same compassion to ourselves. Our inner dialogue is often laced with self-criticism and negative self-talk, a harshness we would never direct at someone we cared about.

Recognizing this pervasive self-loathing is the first step in reversing it. When we become aware of our internal dialogue and how it shapes our sense of self-worth, we open the door to a more compassionate relationship with ourselves. This journey involves challenging our inner critic and offering ourselves the same respect and understanding we extend to others.

Loving ourselves begins with acknowledging—not dismissing—our beauty, both inner and outer. Many of us struggle with a form of body dysmorphia, harshly critical of own our physical appearance and sending waves of negativity toward parts of ourselves that we "hate." It's difficult for any living being to thrive under such constant condemnation. Your body has been a faithful companion throughout your life. Consider each part a marvel of creation: your feet, which have carried you for thousands of miles; your hands, which allow you to create, express, and connect; your eyes, which have taken in countless wonders; your brain, an organ of awe-inspiring complexity. Cultivate a habit of gratitude, consciously appreciating your body as it is rather than seeing it as defective or burdensome.

Cultivating self-love is especially critical for young people growing up in a social media culture saturated with toxic messages. Raj witnessed this with his daughters, who as teenagers were often critical of their physical appearance—disliking their hair, nose, shoulders, height, and skin. He gently encouraged them to view their bodies with kindness, reminding them that our bodies are gifts, worthy of appreciation, not condemnation.

By fostering self-love and body positivity, we build resilience against harmful cultural pressures, empowering ourselves through self-acceptance and compassion. In doing so, we can learn to see the beauty in ourselves, discounting the distorted lens of societal standards and recognizing the inherent worth of simply being human.

WHAT IS LOVE?

Love is the most potent force in the universe; it is, as Thomas Merton wrote, "the only rational act." The suffering we see around us is a plea to manifest love. Our daily intention upon waking should be, "I greet this day with love in my heart." When the heart is full of love, the world is full of beauty.

What is "love," though? Some might call it a feeling or an attitude. We define it as "the unconditional desire for the well-being of the other." We can expand that to "the conscious choice to see, value, and serve the essence of another being, holding their well-being, growth, and flourishing as sacred, without seeking to possess, control, or diminish them."

When you say "I love you," it shouldn't imply a need or expectation. Love should simply mean wanting the best for another, no strings attached. Love is the ultimate truth, the purpose of life, and the key to the universe.

Self-love is the courageous act of turning that love inward. True self-love is more than passion, friendship, or commitment; it's a state of deep compassion and kindness toward oneself. It means engaging in self-care, nurturing your body, mind, and spirit so they remain whole and flourish. It involves honoring your own needs, embracing your imperfections, and treating yourself with the same patience and understanding you would offer to someone you truly cherish, without conditions or judgment.

At the root of anger and sadness lies fear. Fear and love are mutually exclusive; we can either be in a state of love or a state of fear, but never both. When we lose touch with love, we become vulnerable to fear. This can manifest as rage, withdrawal, or any of the classic trauma responses: fight, flight, freeze, fawn, or flop.

HEALING LEADERS PRACTICE
Metta (Loving-Kindness)

In the Buddhist tradition, the primary meaning of love is friendship. Ask yourself: Can I be a friend to myself? What would that feel like?

Metta is the practice of directing loving-kindness to yourself and others—including people you're angry with or who have caused you pain.[1] When you sit in meditation and send loving-kindness to others, you can trust that it will have an effect—if not on them, certainly on you. Research shows that metta practice can influence your neurology, your immunity, and even your biochemistry.[2] When done with full commitment, it can bring about a state of bliss. In the yogic tradition, this is called *ananda*, a blend of love, peace, and joy.

You'll begin by sending love to your inner child—your five-year-old self.

Place your feet on the ground. Rest your right hand on your heart and your left hand on your belly. Close your eyes and take a deep breath.

Like a strong, loving parent, bring to your mind's eye, in front of your heart space, your child self—the person you were at the age of five. This little one might be playful, mischievous, lost, uncertain, or perhaps a little fearful. Let your heart open spontaneously with compassion. Hold this inner child close to your heart. As you breathe, imagine yourself rocking and soothing them. Say to them: *May you be well. May you be happy. May you be free from all suffering. May you be well. May you be happy. May you be free from all suffering. May you be well. May you be happy. May you be free from all suffering.* Visualize your love flowing like a golden-pink light from your heart into theirs, illuminating them from the inside, making them feel calm, happy, and safe. Watch as they begin to smile.

Next, bring into your mind's eye the version of you that exists today. Notice how tired this person is. See the weight of the problems they have experienced and the challenges they face. Let compassion rise as you send loving-kindness to this present-day self. Say to them: *May you be well. May you be happy. May you be free from all suffering. May you be well. May you be happy. May you be free from all suffering.* Take this present self deep into your heart and let them rest safely there.

Now, visualize your future self. Offer this future version of you loving-kindness, so they can step into the future feeling whole and supported. Say to them: *May you be well. May you be happy. May you be from all suffering. May you be well. May you be happy. May you be free from all suffering.* Draw them into your heart, letting them feel seen, cherished, and safe.

Next, bring forth your inner critic—the part of you that tries to keep you safe and make you grow. It can be harsh, but it has good intentions. Give your inner critic a name and form—you may find that it resembles a parent, teacher, or other authority figure—and notice its tension or guardedness. Offer compassion to this part of yourself, and say: *May you be well. May you be happy. May you be free from all suffering. May you be well. May you be happy. May you be free from all suffering.* Gently invite your inner critic into your heart. Let them be softened by kindness.

To complete the metta practice, take a deep breath and let the warmth of your heart radiate out in all directions—to the tips of your fingers and toes and the crown of your head. Imagine your heart expanding until your whole body rests within it. All your cells are aglow with loving-kindness. Take another deep breath. Rub your palms together vigorously to generate warmth, and cup them over your eyes. Slowly open your eyes. Keeping your gaze on your palms, lower your hands to your lap, then gently raise your gaze to return to this moment in time and space. Wiggle your fingers and toes. Once more, rub your palms together, then sweep them over your face, your temples, your entire body. Come awake and feel the metta flowing through you.

What you have just experienced is an ancient and proven practice. Buddhist monks have been known to spend a full year doing this day in and day out. This is how they cleanse the heart.

THE CONSEQUENCES OF NOT LOVING YOURSELF

When we carry unresolved insecurities, fears, or emotional wounds, we often project these struggles outward, manifesting as aggression or hostility. What starts as a personal battle can ripple outward, fueling conflict and affecting countless lives.

Recognizing that external conflicts often reflect our internal turmoil highlights the importance of self-reflection and self-love. By confronting the pain we carry, we lay the foundation for inner peace and enable more compassionate interactions with others. This inward journey is essential to break cycles of violence and conflict on every scale, from individual to global.

Choosing self-love is choosing peace—not only for ourselves, but for everyone whose lives we touch. Without it, we are more likely to engage in self-sabotaging behaviors that undermine our well-being. These can manifest in various ways, such as engaging in negative self-talk or ignoring our emotional and spiritual needs. When we fail to value ourselves, we (consciously or unconsciously) limit our own potential for health, happiness, and growth.

Being at War with Your Body

Loving oneself extends beyond nurturing the mind and emotions; it also means cultivating a respectful and caring relationship with the body. When we engage in unhealthy habits or disregard our physical needs, we are essentially waging war against ourselves. This internal conflict often surfaces through behaviors that undermine our health, whether by neglect, harmful habits, or self-sabotage.

Raj recalls being at war with his body during a decade of smoking, knowingly harming his respiratory system with each puff. Even after he quit, the internal struggle continued in other forms: neglecting mindful eating, not exercising regularly, and too often turning to alcohol as a coping mechanism.

True self-love requires restoring a harmonious relationship with our physical selves. This means making conscious, supportive choices: eating nourishing foods, moving your body, and avoiding substances that harm us. It also means learning to listen: tuning in to our body's signals, respecting its limits, and offering it kindness and care.

By extending love to our physical bodies, we foster a more holistic self-love. This shift leads to greater well-being and a more positive relationship with ourselves and the world, allowing us to live in greater harmony and health.

Rejecting the Love of Others

When people lack self-love, they often engage in self-sabotaging behaviors that reinforce feelings of unworthiness and inhibit deep connection. This goes beyond the familiar idea that we must love ourselves to truly love others. Those who struggle with self-acceptance often harbor a belief that they are unworthy of love and acceptance from others. They think others' affection is based on a false version of themselves, which they cannot maintain. An inner voice whispers, "They only think they love me because they don't know the real me." Once they discover who I truly am, they'll stop loving me. As a result, even when surrounded by genuine love and support, they find it difficult to embrace that love, subconsciously pushing it away out of fear that their perceived flaws will eventually drive it away.

This struggle to accept love creates a painful dynamic: When someone who doesn't love themselves is loved by another, they begin to question the judgment of the person who loves them. They see the love-giver as misguided or flawed, simply for choosing to love someone they see as unlovable.

This results in a vicious cycle and painful isolation. When individuals don't love themselves, they struggle to accept and reciprocate love, leading to emotional distance and strained relationships. In turn, this reinforces their belief that they are unworthy of love, creating a barrier to the intimacy and connection they long for.

Breaking this cycle begins with self-love. Cultivating self-love is essential to nurturing healthy relationships and being able to receive love freely. By learning to accept and love ourselves unconditionally, we create a stable foundation of self-worth, making us more open to embracing the love and support offered by others. When we see our own worth, we not only open ourselves to the joy of receiving love but also deepen the bonds that bring true connection and fulfillment into our lives.

HEALING LEADERS PRACTICE
Release Your Inner Critic

This exercise is designed to help you recognize the voice of your inner critic. For most of us, this is a powerful voice that whispers, "You're not enough. You don't have enough. You're not good enough." These messages can hold you back, keeping you from flourishing and finding happiness.

Imagine these thoughts as knots that bind your heart, mind, and spirit. Only by acknowledging them can you begin to untie them. Recognizing your inner critic is like retrieving something long hidden in the basement of your psyche. Bring it into the light, air it out, and gently, compassionately release it.

To connect with your inner critic, start by listing five things you don't love about yourself.

Next, list five things you think others don't love about you.

Finally, write down five things you haven't forgiven yourself for.

What was it like to hear the voice of your inner critic and see its messages in your own words? Hold these thoughts lightly, with the intention of letting them go. Don't take them as truths—they are simply habits of thought that you can choose to let go.

Working with your inner critic begins with self-love. Another helpful practice is activating your *inner coach*—the part of you that says, "You've got this. You're enough. I believe in you. We're in this together." The next time you hear a negative voice in your head, recognize it as your inner critic, not your higher self. Step back and replace it with your inner coach's voice of encouragement.

CULTIVATE SELF-ACCEPTANCE AND SELF-LOVE

Your first and most important relationship is the one you have with yourself. If that relationship is unhealthy, it distorts every other aspect of your life. Breaking the cycle of self-doubt and insecurity begins with cultivating self-acceptance and self-love. True spiritual growth starts here—not with mere tolerance or reluctant acceptance, but with a wholehearted embrace of who you are.

The journey toward self-love demands patience, self-compassion, and the courage to challenge deep-seated negative beliefs. As we come to recognize our own inherent worth, our relationships—both with ourselves and others—begin to flourish, becoming more fulfilling and authentic.

Begin by simply accepting: *This seems to be who I am. Let me start from here.* Without self-acceptance, self-love cannot take root. The paradox is that only by accepting ourselves as who we are can we evolve and grow.

Self-love goes beyond acceptance; it is a profound celebration of the miracle of our existence. We did not create ourselves; we have been gifted with extraordinary minds, bodies, and imaginations that we did nothing to earn. Within each of us lies a marvel shaped by 4.5 billion years of evolution: a mind more powerful than any human-made computer inside a body that heals and adapts with astonishing sophistication, and an imagination capable of dreaming beyond the stars.

When we truly grasp the magnitude of this gift, failing to love ourselves becomes an act of profound ingratitude. This life we have been given is nothing short of a treasure—one deserving our utmost care, respect, and appreciation.

Self-love is about honoring our intrinsic worth—not because of our achievements or how others see us, but simply because we exist. This love extends to every part of ourselves: physical, mental, emotional, and spiritual. It's about nurturing ourselves, recognizing our place in the vast, interconnected web of life, and seeing ourselves as valuable pieces of a much greater whole.

Christine Dyer, a participant in a Shakti Leadership workshop we led at the Esalen Institute, responded to a question with a deep insight before spontaneously exclaiming, "I am so in awe of myself right now!" We should all take such delight in what our minds and bodies are capable of manifesting—without slipping into narcissism, of course!

Embracing self-love is not an act of selfishness or vanity but a humble recognition of the sacred gift that is life. By cherishing and celebrating ourselves, we honor the universe's long, beautiful journey that has brought us here. We open ourselves to a life rich with joy, fulfillment, and connection—an existence that reflects the love we discover within.

HEALING LEADERS PRACTICE
Write a Love Letter to Yourself

Writing a love letter to yourself is an act of self-compassion that strengthens your connection to your body and spirit. Begin by finding a peaceful space where you can sit comfortably. Take a few deep breaths to bring your attention to the present moment. Reflect on your journey—consider the challenges you've faced, the victories you've celebrated, and the simple, everyday moments you've savored. Your body has been your steadfast companion through it all.

Address yourself warmly: "Dear [Your Name]," and write as if speaking to a cherished friend. Express gratitude for all that your body has done for you—your feet that carry you forward, your hands that create and comfort, your heart that loves and endures. Acknowledge any parts of yourself that you have been critical of, offering them kindness and understanding. Say, "I know I haven't always appreciated you as you deserve, but today, I choose to honor and cherish you."

Celebrate your unique qualities, embracing your resilience, laughter, and warmth. Affirm your worth: "I am enough, just as I am. I am worthy of love, compassion, and joy." Commit to caring for your body and spirit as you go forward, promising to listen, nurture, and treat yourself with kindness.

Close your letter, "With love and gratitude, [Your Name]." Place your hand on your heart and read it aloud, taking deep, grounding breaths and letting the words resonate within you. Keep this letter close as a reminder of your worth and the love you carry within. This practice shifts the inner dialogue from self-criticism to self-compassion, nurturing a more profound sense of self-appreciation and connection.

TAKE CARE OF YOURSELF

Self-care isn't selfish; it's the foundation for everything else we give to the world. As the actress Glenn Close once said, "We have to do the work to keep our glass—our beings, our soul, our heart—full, and then we deal with the world using the overflow."[3]

Nilima shares:

> *In my ten-plus years as a cancer coach, witnessing burned-out caregivers became routine. It was clear that a lack of self-care on the part of the patient often contributed to the weakening of their immune system. But what struck me even more was the not-so-uncommon phenomenon of codependence: caregivers becoming entangled in the patient's unconscious self-depleting patterns and falling sick themselves.*
>
> *I often had to coach caregivers using the familiar airline metaphor: "Put your own oxygen mask on first before helping others." I understood this lesson not just professionally, but personally. When my husband was diagnosed with colon cancer at age forty, I became his primary caregiver—and in the process, I lost myself.*
>
> *It took two decades and a deep spiritual practice, rooted in the path of the integral yogini, for me to finally see that true service requires self-love. I needed to care for myself first—not in a way that abandoned my dharma to my loved ones, but in a way that allowed me to honor it more fully. It wasn't until 2022 that I fully stepped into this realization. By then, I had fulfilled my responsibilities: my husband was a healthy sixty-year-old, and both my son (thirty-two) and my daughter (twenty-nine) were emotionally and financially independent.*
>
> *Loving myself meant I could now move on—with a clear conscience—to grow along the path of my soul's calling. Staying any longer risked making me sick with soul-grief from a suppressed purpose. Needless to say, leaving a thirty-four-year marriage took everything I had. But it began with the hardest and most important act of all: choosing to truly love myself.*

Self-love is a term that unpacks into self-acceptance and self-care. Self-acceptance is the act of embracing who you truly are, while self-care is the expression of that acceptance through loving action. To care for yourself is to honor your body, emotions, mind, soul, and spirit—an active demonstration of self-love.

Think of self-care as "paying yourself first." If possible, set aside 5 to 10 percent of your year and 10 percent of each day for self-care. This amounts to three to five weeks annually and about two hours each day. For instance, Raj renews his vitality each year by spending three weeks at an Ayurvedic healing retreat in South India—a powerful reset for his body, mind, and spirit. Additionally, he dedicates a part of his mornings to practices like yoga, meditation, strength training, and aerobic exercise, building a strong foundation for the day.

Self-care doesn't always require big commitments; it can be woven into the smallest moments. Take a breath, feel the oxygen provided by the trees around you, and allow yourself to reset. Set up self-care reminders on your phone: Every two hours, pause to stretch, breathe deeply, or simply connect with yourself. These mini-breaks may seem small, but they bring tremendous benefits to your well-being.

Nilima's self-care practice illustrates how powerful these moments can be. When she lived in Ajijic, Mexico, she had a terrace with breathtaking views of mountains on one side and a lake on the other. Whenever her body felt tense, she would step outside, letting the sunlight and the scenery soothe her. She would spend five minutes with the sun on her face, affirming, "I'm back in my body. I'm breathing again. My mind feels good." Each morning, she greeted the sun, imagining her cells as little smileys, absorbing the light and filling her with joy. At sunset, she would take in the beauty as the sun dipped into the lake, nurturing herself through the simplicity of nature's rhythm.

Self-care is about creating small, meaningful rituals that reconnect you to your essence. Stepping outside for fresh air, feeling the sun's warmth, moving your body—these practices are powerful acts of self-love that nourish and ground you, helping you approach life with greater balance, joy, and resilience.

LOVE AND HEAL YOUR WOUNDED INNER CHILD

When we look closely at the early lives of history's most tyrannical figures, a powerful thread emerges: Each carried a wounded "inner child." Scarred by deep emotional wounds and unresolved trauma, their unmet needs and unhealed pain surfaced later in life as destructive behaviors.

The violence, hatred, and cruelty that have plagued humanity for centuries reflect this unhealed inner suffering. When people cannot face and heal their inner turmoil, their pain festers, seeking an outlet. Anger and hurt are projected outward, fueling cycles of conflict that reverberate through families, communities, and even nations.

Recognizing this pattern highlights the urgent need to address our own childhood traumas. External conflict often stems from internal wounds. Healing begins by confronting the pain within, acknowledging the unfulfilled needs of our younger selves, and offering the compassion we may never have received. Through self-reflection, therapy, and the support of compassionate others, we can start breaking these cycles of pain.

Healing one's wounded inner child requires commitment to self-reflection, self-compassion, and deep inner work. By learning to listen to and nurture this vulnerable part of ourselves, we replace self-blame with understanding and resentment with forgiveness. We come to see that our pain does not define us; it simply marks where love and care were absent.

When we embrace our wounded inner child with kindness, we transform our relationships not only with ourselves but also with others. As we heal, we foster inner harmony that radiates outward, making compassion and peace more possible in all our interactions. In this way, inner healing creates a ripple effect, helping build a world that values understanding over judgment, compassion over conflict, and healing over harm.

HEALING LEADERS PRACTICE
Heal Your Inner Child

Healing your inner child is a powerful practice that fosters self-compassion and deepens your sense of wholeness. Begin by finding a quiet, comfortable space and closing your eyes. Take a few deep breaths to ground

yourself and bring to mind an image of yourself as a young child, around five years old. Picture this child standing before you, their emotions and needs visible. Notice if they seem scared, lonely, or in need of comfort, and let your heart fill with compassion.

Place your hand over your heart and, with gentle reassurance, speak to your inner child: "I see you and know what you've been through. You are safe now. You are loved just as you are." Envision holding this child, offering warmth and safety as light radiates from your heart, enveloping you both in a soothing glow.

Repeat loving affirmations: "You are worthy of love and happiness. Your feelings are valid, and you are never alone." Allow these words to resonate deeply as you embrace your inner child, so they feel heard, seen, and cherished. Gradually, imagine this child merging with you, becoming a part of your present self. Feel their presence within you, now safe and at peace.

Place both hands on your heart and close the practice with gratitude: "I am whole, I am loved, and I am at peace." Slowly return your awareness to the present, wiggling your fingers and toes, and open your eyes when ready. By repeating this practice regularly, you build a lasting bond with your inner child, healing past wounds and nurturing a compassionate relationship with yourself.

THE POWER OF AFFIRMATIONS

Affirmations are powerful statements that tap into the healing power of language. When spoken with intention, they resonate deeply within the mind and body. The body listens to our words, internalizing them as beliefs, allowing affirmations to transform our inner landscape.

Meridian therapies, inspired by the ancient Chinese system of energy pathways, offer a unique way to enhance affirmations. These pathways, or meridians, guide energy flow throughout the body, with eight main meridians accessible at the "karate chop point"—the base of the outer edge of the hand, just above the wrist.[4]

To amplify the power of your affirmations, gently tap this karate chop point while you speak. You can tap either hand or alternate between them, allowing the movement to release blockages in your energy body. As you do, you're not only speaking new beliefs into being but also actively clearing away old, limiting ones.

Speak the following affirmations aloud while tapping the karate chop point:

> I accept, embrace, and am deeply grateful for all my innate qualities. These are gifts I have received.
>
> Even though parts of myself are still growing and healing, I accept and honor those aspects as part of my journey.
>
> I am grateful for my body, every part of it.
>
> I am a unique being, here to contribute to the world in ways only I can.

After finishing the affirmations, rub your hands together, place them on your heart, and breathe slowly, focusing on each chakra (energy center) in turn:

1. Inhale at the crown of your head, exhale.
2. Inhale at the third eye, exhale.
3. Inhale at the throat, exhale.
4. Inhale at the heart, exhale.
5. Inhale at the solar plexus, exhale.
6. Inhale below the navel, exhale.
7. Inhale at the tailbone, exhale.

When you're ready, open your eyes, bringing a sense of calm and integration with you. By embracing this practice, you are both affirming new beliefs and allowing the energy within you to realign and support the vision you hold for yourself.

CONSCIOUS LEADERS SPEAK
Love Yourself

To lead others with love, we must first learn to lead ourselves that way. Yet self-love can be elusive—overshadowed by perfectionism, performance, trauma, or conditioning. For the conscious leaders we interviewed, learning to love themselves was not an egoic act, but a sacred one. Their stories illuminate how the capacity for self-love is born of honesty, healing, and sometimes heartbreak.

For Kip Tindell, self-love was not hard-won—it was natural, because it was nurtured. His story reminds us what becomes possible when the soil of early life is rich with love. "I was raised by two wonderful parents who gave me unconditional love. I didn't have to work for their approval—it was just there. I think that makes it easier to love yourself. I'm happy to say I genuinely like who I am. I'm still learning, still growing—but I'm comfortable in my own skin. Myself and I are friends."

Avivah Wittenberg-Cox, a thought leader on generational balance and gender dynamics, was shaped by a mother who survived Auschwitz and yet chose joy. "After what she'd lived through, my mother still came back joyful, and that energy shaped me. I've never felt the need to overcompensate or overperform to be lovable. Self-love, for me, was largely inherited. But I've also deepened it by choosing work and relationships that feel aligned. That kind of congruence reinforces love—when your outer world reflects your inner values."

Marisa Lazo was profoundly shaped by her father's bipolar disorder—as well as his unconditional love. "My father adored me. Even though he was very sick—at times hospitalized—I always felt loved by him. From a young age, I learned to love both the dark and the light in people. As I started to know myself better, I loved myself better. You build inner strength by embracing the totality of your experience—not just the good parts. Having loving-kindness for yourself doesn't mean always feeling happy; it means taking time to reflect, to ask: Where am I grasping? Where am I not accepting? Where can I let go?"

Doug Rauch describes a turning point moment of healing through unconditional acceptance. "When I was seventeen, I asked my dad, 'Why don't you like me?' He said, 'I don't know. I just don't.' That could have devastated me. But by then I had met Swami Prabhupadananda, a spiritual teacher who accepted me fully—holes in my jeans and all. That love healed something fundamental in me. Self-love isn't about pride—it's about wholeness. It's being able to sit with your own essence and know you're enough. When you get to that place, love overflows. You stop needing to fix others. You just start loving them."

For Gervase Warner, self-love wasn't a dramatic breakthrough, but a gradual progression. "I didn't struggle with self-loathing, but I did spend years asking, 'Am I good enough?' Was I smart enough, funny enough? There was always a comparison running in the background. My mother used to say I was selfish—and I just accepted that. But over the years, I've softened. The voice of judgment isn't as loud anymore."

Simon Cohen reveals the cost of pushing through life without pause—and the power of self-kindness. "My father never said, 'Congratulations.' Even when I won the national championship, he said, 'The good swimmers weren't there.' That drive made me who I am—but it also burned me." Simon is learning to listen to his body and care for himself more. "Recently, I was supposed to fly to Monterrey for an important meeting, but my back was killing me. Ten years ago, I would have gone anyway. But I listened to my body and canceled. That pain was my body saying, 'Love me. Rest me.' Choosing to listen was an act of love."

Kristin Engvig discovered self-love not as a feeling, but as a set of daily rituals that saved her life. "I gave so much to others, always saying yes. Although I had more freedom than most people, I realized I was not as free as I thought when my overwork caused burnout. I didn't use my deep intuition and my wisdom sufficiently on myself. My willpower could override my own needs, feelings, and intuition, even if I could see it in others. I began taking my personal practice to a new level and created sacred structures—one day off per week, long walks, yoga, rest. After ninety days, it became part of me. It saved me. I started to feel healthier. Then I felt more worthy. And then I saw—it's not just about me. Loving myself is a gift to the world."

Morad Fareed's journey required him to break down completely before he could begin to build love from within. "My nature is maternal—caring, sensitive, poetic. But I grew up in a hyper-masculine, Type-A Palestinian family. At some point, I overadapted. I lost myself. I burned myself into smithereens—spiritually, physically, emotionally. The reason I was suffering was because I wasn't being myself. My body literally said, 'I won't live this lie anymore.' That's when the journey to self-love began—not from triumph, but from surrender."

Despite extraordinary outward success, John Mackey wrestled privately with feelings of unworthiness for much of his life. "I grew up with a very critical father. I internalized the belief that I had to be perfect to be loved. And since I was never perfect, I concluded I wasn't lovable. Even when people expressed love for me, I assumed they didn't really know me. But during a guided spiritual journey in 2022, I experienced unconditional love—for myself, for existence, for God. I cried and cried. That was the first time I truly felt that I am worthy of love—not for what I do, but for who I am." John's core message throughout our conversation was about the primacy of love—unconditional, expansive, healing. "Love is who we are. When we return to that truth, everything else falls into place."

For Timothy Henry, the absence of early love shaped a life mission: to learn to love well. "There was no secure attachment in my early life. No holding. I went from hospital to orphanage to foster care to abuse. That creates a deep wound. Loving myself has been a lifelong journey. It's not what I received, but what I've had to learn to give. I made it my purpose: to love well. Becoming a father gave me the chance to reparent myself. I poured into my kids what I never got. I said to myself: It ends here. This cycle of harm ends with me."

Each of these leaders took a different path toward self-love. Some were blessed with it early. Others had to reclaim it through breakdown, reflection, ritual, or reparenting. All of them remind us: to love yourself is not narcissism—it is spiritual hygiene. It is what allows us to lead not from wounds, but from wholeness.

By completing this chapter on learning to love yourself, you've laid a strong foundation of self-compassion, acceptance, and care. But self-love is not just an end in itself—it's also a gateway to deeper transformation. When you truly embrace who you are, flaws and all, you unlock the courage to live more authentically.

The journey of loving yourself prepares you for the next essential step: *being* yourself. It's one thing to recognize and accept your inner qualities, and another to express them freely and confidently in the world. In the next chapter, we'll explore how to live from this place of authenticity—how to align your actions, choices, and relationships with who you truly are.

CHAPTER 4

Be Your Self

When you are content
to be simply yourself and
don't compare or compete,
everyone will respect you.

—LAO TZU

After getting to know yourself and love yourself, the next step is to fully *be* yourself. This is about resting comfortably within your being, free from the pressure to act, impress, or conform. Too often, we adopt roles or personas that aren't authentic to our true essence. We adapt ourselves for work, relationships, or social acceptance—but if these adaptations don't align with our inner truth, they won't bring fulfillment or peace.

Strive to embody your essence—both within yourself and in the unique presence you bring to the world. This doesn't mean ignoring areas where you want to grow; instead, it means fully inhabiting your core qualities. If you are naturally trusting, peaceful, or idealistic (like Raj), embrace these qualities. Radiate them. To be yourself is to live in alignment with the gifts you were born with, rather than suppressing them to fit someone else's ideals.

Holding back who you are is a loss, not only for you, but also for the world. Your strengths, qualities, and passions are meant to be shared in a loving way. We often "weaponize" our strengths, using intelligence or wit, for example, to criticize or hurt others. But these same qualities can become healing forces. Imagine your strengths as instruments of love rather than defense or attack, bringing comfort, inspiration, and joy to those around you.

Each of us must remember who we are and express that identity with humble confidence. In doing so, we contribute to the greater symphony of humanity, in which each person's unique essence plays a vital part.

Brother David Steindl-Rast shares a story from Jewish mysticism, in which a master prays, "Make me like Abraham." The voice from heaven replies, "I already have an Abraham. I want you."[1] Each of us is here to be our unique self, not an imperfect copy of someone else. The world needs the real you.

Find your voice, identify your unique gifts, and use them to serve the greatest good. As Nilima puts it, "You are homeless if you're not residing in your higher self." To be truly at home in yourself, tune out the noise of external pressures—parental expectations, societal standards, peer influence—and turn up the volume on your own heart and soul. The idiom "march to the beat of your own drum" fits well here: It's about living your own way, not according to society's norms or expectations.

Being yourself means feeling completely at home within your own skin. It's a journey to "un-become" everything you're not, so you can step fully into who you are.

Being yourself is an act of service, not selfishness. We each carry a unique piece of the puzzle that is needed to complete the picture of the world as it is meant to be. When we show up fully as ourselves, we inspire others to do the same. Be yourself in a way that overflows with generosity and compassion. Make yourself an offering to the world.

STOP ACTING! EMBRACE AUTHENTICITY

When you learn who you are and come to love yourself as you would a precious friend, you unlock one of life's greatest freedoms: the freedom to show up as your real, authentic self. To be yourself is not merely an ideal; it is the ultimate act of self-respect. It means stepping fully into the world, unhesitatingly, unapologetically, and offering your truth through your actions, words, and decisions. It is the conscious choice to live in alignment with your innermost essence.

Most of us adopt different personas depending on the context. We are one way with our parents, another with our kids. We show up differently with the people we lead than with the people who lead us. We behave differently with our friends than we do with our colleagues. All this role-playing is exhausting and unnecessary. Strive to be the same person in every setting: your authentic self.

Give yourself permission to release old patterns and identities. Let go of the versions of yourself others have come to expect, of the masks you may have worn for others' comfort or approval. To truly be yourself, you must shed these layers of expectation and unburden yourself of roles that no longer fit. In this process of detachment, you are invited to simply *be*—to rest in the pure, timeless presence that is your essence, beyond gender, race, religion, nationality, or any other label. It is not only permissible but essential to detach from these surface-level identities and discover the beauty of just *being*.

Imagine this process of un-becoming as a "reset to factory settings." It's a conscious choice to release outdated patterns and welcome in a new, authentic way of being. This is self-liberating, a powerful declaration that you are worthy of living from your deepest truth.

The path of authenticity, while deeply rewarding, calls for courage. It requires embracing vulnerability and, at times, exposing parts of yourself that are tender and raw. Nilima has observed this courage in Raj, who models what it means to "be himself" during his healing retreats for leaders. His willingness to share personal, sometimes painful, stories creates a profound sense of connection and trust within the group. In spaces where vulnerability is not usually welcomed—classrooms, corporate settings, and workshops—Raj's openness sets the tone, inviting others to lower their shields and risk showing up exactly as they are.

Creating a Culture of Authenticity

To be yourself is to understand that you are enough as you are. It is to recognize that the highest form of leadership is modeling the very vulnerability and authenticity we long to see in the world. In having the courage to be yourself, you not only fulfill your own deepest calling but invite others to do the same, creating a culture where each person can show up fully, confidently, and without fear.

Authenticity in leadership is not simply a matter of personal preference, but a profound responsibility. When a leader stands openly and authentically, revealing their own truths, showing up with both their strengths and their wounds, others feel safe to do the same. By setting a standard of openness, they pave the way for a culture that values truth, that allows people to express, explore, and evolve.

Raj exemplifies this. In choosing to lead with presence and vulnerability, he helps create a conscious culture—one rooted in trust, openness, and care. It's not just about professional collaboration; it becomes a space for deep personal growth, where people are supported in discovering themselves, loving themselves, and honoring their own worth. When leaders dare to be themselves, they create a ripple effect of authenticity, inspiring those around them to do the same.

As a leader, you set the bar; you shape the culture. If you reach an eight out of ten in openness, others will feel comfortable rising to a six or a seven. But if you're only at a three, no one will rise above a two.

Sacrificing Authenticity for Attachment

"The Dangers of the Good Child," a thought-provoking article published by The School of Life, features a surprising warning about children who seem to embody every parent's dream.[2] These are the children who always do their homework, keep their rooms spotless, and never break rules. While such behavior might appear ideal on the surface, this "perfect" exterior often masks important underlying issues.

It's important to understand why these children are so well-behaved. Their flawless conduct frequently develops as a response to challenging family dynamics—perhaps to support a depressed parent who can't handle any additional stress, to avoid triggering an angry parent's outbursts, or to capture the attention of a distant caregiver who might otherwise overlook them entirely. As the article states, "The secret sorrows—and future difficulties—of the good boy or girl begin with their inner need for excessive compliance."

This pattern of excessive compliance sets the stage for significant challenges in adulthood. These individuals often grow up struggling to express their true thoughts and feelings, bottling up emotions until they manifest as physical symptoms or sudden outbursts. Their childhood conditioning in being "good" leaves them ill-equipped for adult life's complexities, particularly in areas like intimate relationships and career development. They might find themselves unable to advocate for their needs, set boundaries, or challenge others' opinions—skills that are crucial for personal and professional success.

At the core of these difficulties lies a crucial missing piece in their emotional development. Unlike children who occasionally misbehave but know that they're still loved, these "good children" never experience the fundamental reassurance that they can be imperfect—even "bad"—and still be worthy of acceptance and love. This leaves them with a fragile sense of self-worth tied exclusively to their ability to please others.

Children like these, and the adults they become, are unable to be themselves for fear of being rejected by parents, friends, or others they care about. They sacrifice their authenticity for the sake of maintaining their attachments and receiving the acceptance, approval, and love of others.

Says Nilima:

As the younger of two, I watched my sister embody the perfect "good child." She regularly came home first in her class in the early school years, proudly wearing a gold star on her blouse. Even as a somewhat clueless child, I sensed something important: My mother loved her for it. Somewhere in my four-year-old heart, a limiting and self-sabotaging belief took root—"I will be loved if I am better." That belief quietly launched a lifelong quest to be the best, as I subconsciously felt that love from my mother, my source of emotional security, depended on it.

This belief had a double-edged effect. On one hand, it jolted me out of my early passivity and turned me into a high achiever. But on the other hand, it planted the seeds of a painful sibling rivalry for our parents' love and attention—something I neither wanted nor enjoyed. I deeply loved my sister and didn't want to compete with her. I felt trapped in a dynamic of comparison that pitted us against each other, when all I longed for was connection and belonging. (As a footnote, I am happy to report that with some heart-broken-open truth-telling, I have been able to reconcile with her. Sometimes it takes a lifetime to be able to speak and hear such truths. A lot depends on your ability to communicate in a nonviolent way, and on others being emotionally ready to hear what you have to say, and to love you more than they fear facing painful truths.)

PRESENCE—THE MASTER KEY TO BEING YOURSELF

Truly being oneself begins with cultivating presence. Presence is the foundation, the essential grounding that enables us to move beyond the confines of ego and into the vastness of our true essence. Think of it as the master key: It opens the door to conscious leadership, personal healing, and authentic living. With presence, we rest comfortably in who we are—anchored, unshaken, and deeply connected to our core.

Presence is a state of profound awareness and constant, conscious communion with our higher self. It invites us to turn inward and discover the boundless intelligence and insight that lie within.

In this inner stillness, we tap into the source of our deepest power: a power that guides our choices and shapes our impact.

When we lead from presence, we become a vessel for something greater than ourselves. There is no forcing, no struggle—only a natural unfolding. Presence transforms us from within. It teaches us to live with open eyes and open hearts, to face life directly and courageously. It is not just a tool for leadership; it is the path to becoming completely, authentically alive.

To be present is to fully inhabit the moment, embracing it with a deep awareness that anchors us in the here and now. It's a state of conscious flow, where balance, completeness, connection, and contentment converge, in sync with the rhythms of life. Presence is not a place of tense alertness, but relaxed concentration—an attunement to all that is within and around us.

Unfortunately, most of the time, we are not present. Our bodies are in one place, while our minds are elsewhere—lost in memories of the past or anxieties about the future. We exist in fragments, seldom meeting life where it actually happens: in the present moment. The present is all we really have. The future is yet to be, and the past is no more. Only *this* moment offers us the chance to see clearly, respond wisely, and manifest our truest intentions.

What does it feel like to inhabit this rarefied state? Imagine standing in the eye of a storm, calm, centered, and fully aware, as chaos swirls around you. You are both grounded and expansive, able to meet each moment exactly as it is. For leaders, this is especially vital. Life brings a constant stream of challenges, and only presence allows us to respond with clarity, resilience, and grace.

Conscious leadership is impossible without presence. A leader must not only appear calm but genuinely embody it. This calmness creates a psychologically safe space around them, inviting others to bring their best selves forward and relax into their potential.

Achieving this state takes practice—what in yoga is called *sadhana*, a disciplined commitment. Yet over time, presence becomes second nature, an inner state that remains accessible even in the most challenging circumstances.

HEALING LEADERS PRACTICE
Cultivate a State of Presence

This practice, adapted from the work of Conscious Leadership coaches Vijay Bhat and Hank Fieger, offers a pathway back to presence—a quick, accessible approach for those who feel rushed, overwhelmed, or distracted. Let it be a doorway back to yourself, a means to rediscover the calm within.

RELAXED BODY

We begin with the foundation of presence: a relaxed body, open and grounded. Settle into a chair, letting it support you fully. Close your eyes and plant your feet firmly on the ground, as if you were drawing strength from the earth itself. Let your head, neck, and shoulders soften, with your spine straight yet supple. Rest your hands on your thighs, palms up or down. Now, surrender any tightness you're carrying, layer by layer.

Start with your face. Tighten every muscle, from your forehead to your scalp, feeling the pull in your cheeks and jaw. Squeeze, hold, then release. Let go so completely that you feel your face fall into softness, as if you're melting into ease. Now move to your shoulders and arms, tightening, squeezing your fists, holding all the tension—and then release it. Feel the weight drop from your shoulders and your hands and arms relax. Next, tighten your torso, drawing your ribcage and abdominal muscles inward, contracting your belly, gathering all the stress that hides there—and then release it, letting your core soften and expand. Move down, tightening your hips, thighs, knees, calves, and feet, curling your toes inward—hold, and then release, sending the tension out through your feet and into the earth.

Finally, take a deep, cleansing breath. As you inhale, feel your whole body filling with fresh, cool air, from the crown of your head all the way to the tips of your toes. As you exhale, feel any lingering tension dissolve, leaving you with a profound sense of relaxation. Your body is now a quiet vessel, ready to receive presence.

EVEN BREATH

With your body relaxed, shift your focus to the next doorway into presence: your breath. We have long known that our emotional state impacts the quality of our breathing; we have also learned that we can consciously use our breath to shift our emotional state. Notice the natural rhythm of your breathing, letting yourself become acutely aware of each inhalation and exhalation. Is it smooth or jagged? Shallow or deep? Without judgment, guide it gently toward balance and evenness, making each breath a little longer, a little fuller.

Inhale slowly, feeling your ribcage lift and your belly expand like a balloon. Then release, exhaling fully and letting your chest drop as your lungs empty completely. Again, inhale, chest rising, belly filling—and exhale, releasing every bit of air. Continue at your own pace, finding a rhythm that feels both natural and calming. Think of your breath as an infinite loop, with no beginning or end. With each breath, you grow more centered, anchored in the here and now. Your breath is the bridge, connecting your body to your spirit, grounding you in presence.

CLEAR MIND AND OPEN HEART

Now, with body and breath in harmony, you are ready to clear your mind and open your heart. Imagine your mind as a pristine mountain lake on a warm summer day. The surface of this lake is perfectly still, untouched by even the faintest breeze. There are no ripples, just crystal-clear water reflecting the vast blue sky. This is your mind in its purest state—calm, transparent, serene.

Approach this lake within you, and gaze at the reflection of your face in its surface. Look closely. What do you see? Notice the calm in your eyes, the quiet in your expression. Your whole being is still and at peace, as if time itself has paused for you. Now, step forward and enter this lake of stillness. Feel the water envelop you, its coolness refreshing and gentle. With each step, go deeper, sinking into its healing embrace, until the water reaches your heart.

Bring your awareness to your physical heart. Feel its steady beat, a rhythm that has been with you since you were just a cluster of cells in your mother's womb. Tirelessly pulsing life into every cell of your body, this faithful companion has powered you through joys and sorrows, through beauty and heartbreak. Offer your heart silent thanks for every moment it has carried you, every beat that has kept you alive and present in this world. Feel a deep sense of gratitude just for being in this moment, able to experience the miracle of life.

Now, allow your awareness to go even deeper, connecting to your emotional heart. Feel it expand, opening beyond the boundaries of your own body. Imagine it radiating warmth and light, reaching outward to encompass the people around you, those you know and those you don't. Let it expand further, extending throughout your neighborhood, your city, your country, and beyond, connecting with all life across the world. Feel the pulse of humanity, of all beings, merging with your own. Sense the oneness of all spirit—a vast field of energy that unites every living thing.

In this state, you have moved beyond the surface of ordinary consciousness into a profound state of pure being. Your body is relaxed, your breath even, your mind clear, and your heart open. Here, you are fully present, connected to everything yet unburdened by anything. You are both whole and part of a larger whole, anchored in the timeless flow of existence.

THE AFFIRMATIONS

Begin by bringing your attention to your gut, the center of your lower abdomen. This is where we hold our most primal instincts, the seat of self-protection and defense. It's also where new human life is created. Here lies deep vulnerability, where we often brace ourselves in anticipation of attack or judgment. Gently place your awareness here, and affirm to yourself: The reality of this moment is that I have nothing to defend. Allow this truth to resonate deeply within your gut. Breathe into your belly, softening any tension. With each inhale, allow ease to enter; with each exhale, releasing the grip of old fears. Let your gut relax as it comes to know this truth: you are safe, and there is nothing to guard against in this moment. Feel a new sense of openness emerge.

Now, move your awareness up to your heart, the tender place within us that so often craves approval, validation, and love. From here, we seek to win others over, to sell our ideas, our worth, our identity. Gently acknowledge this impulse, and offer yourself the gift of release. Affirm softly: The reality of this moment is that I have nothing to promote. Let this truth settle in your heart. As you breathe into it, feel the relief of not needing to prove yourself to anyone. You are whole, you are enough, just as you are. Rest comfortably in your own being, free from the pull of external validation.

Next, bring your focus to your mind, the space where fears are born and often take root. The mind conjures anxieties about the future, fixates on worries of "what if," and spins scenarios that may never come to pass. Settle into the present moment, and affirm with clarity: The reality of this moment is that I have nothing to fear. Breathe deeply, letting this truth sink into your mind. Release the grip of anxious thoughts about the future or regrets from the past. There is no future to fret over, no past to relive—only this calm, grounded present, where there is no danger, no shadow, only peace.

Now bring your awareness to your whole being. Feel the alignment of these centers—gut, heart, and mind—drawing you into a profound state of presence. Affirm slowly: The only reality . . . of this moment . . . is that . . . I am . . . here . . . now. Let this truth ripple through your entire body, from the crown of your head to the tips of your toes, anchoring itself along your spine, the column of your being. Feel yourself solidly grounded in this timeless present, where your truest essence resides.

Now, envision a river of radiant light flowing down from above, renewing you and filling you with boundless energy. Imagine this powerful, luminous stream descending through the crown of your head, down your spine, nourishing every cell, every organ, as it flows through you. Let it irrigate your body and mind, energizing you from within. Any excess energy flows down through your feet, grounding you further as you become a channel for this universal force. Imagine it coursing into the earth, nourishing the ground beneath you, connecting you to the whole of life. As you feel this energy, affirm: Everything I need is within me. Everything I need comes to me. Everything I need flows through me. I am fully in service to that which seeks to emerge into the world through my being in this present moment.

Close with these final affirmations, each a timeless truth of your being: I am enough. I have enough. There is enough for all to share. Let these words settle into every part of your being, dispelling the inner voices that perpetuate scarcity, self-doubt, and insecurity. Feel your wholeness, your completeness, and the abundance that surrounds and connects us all.

Now rub your palms together to generate warmth, and gently massage your forehead, your temples, your cheeks. Rub your palms together again and cup them over your eyes. Slowly open your eyes and, keeping your gaze on your palms, gently lower your hands to rest on your thighs. Then lift your gaze back to the space you are in, now fully in your presence.

These affirmations are designed to counter the ways we habitually lose presence, to soothe the inner voices that tell us that we are not enough, that there is never enough. These are the mantras to return to whenever doubt, fear, or judgment arises.

SUMMARY OF AFFIRMATIONS

I have nothing to defend.

I have nothing to promote.

I have nothing to fear.

I am here now.

All I need is within me.

All I need comes to me.

All I need flows through me.

I am in service to that which seeks to emerge.

I am enough.

I have enough.

There is enough for everyone.

Use this practice as needed in situations that require your full presence, such as an important meeting or a speech in front of a large audience. You will experience an immediate shift in your state of being, from being absent and anxious to being present and fully in service to the moment.

Over time, strive to make presence your default state. Begin with five minutes a day, sitting quietly in stillness, cultivating this inner calm, anchoring in the now. Let this practice expand naturally to ten minutes, then fifteen. Over time, presence will weave itself into the fabric of who you are, becoming an effortless way of being. It will feel as natural to you

as breathing—a steady, grounding current in all you do. In this state, you become a beacon of calm and a catalyst for positive change. This is the natural state of a truly conscious leader.

ESCAPE MENTAL CONFINES

To be yourself, you have to free yourself, shedding the limiting beliefs you've consciously or unconsciously accepted about who you are.

In India, elephants are often domesticated to assist humans with heavy labor. The training begins early, when the elephant is still a calf. The young elephant is chained to a sturdy tree, which it is far too small and weak to uproot. Day after day, it pulls at the chain, struggling against its confinement, but each time, it finds itself held firmly in place. Over time, it learns that resistance is futile and eventually stops pulling. Even as it grows into a powerful adult, capable of uprooting trees with a single tug, it remains bound by the same chain. By then, the chain is no longer attached to the tree, yet the elephant doesn't attempt to move. The chain around its leg has become a mental boundary, an invisible prison of its own making. It believes freedom is beyond its reach, so it never even considers breaking free.

This is the nature of the mental confines we often find ourselves trapped within—beliefs, assumptions, and limitations that once may have served a purpose but now only hold us back. Gay Hendricks refers to this as the "upper limit problem," the unconscious barriers we place on ourselves that restrict our happiness, success, and growth.[3] These barriers are invisible, but they are as binding as chains. We are taught from a young age to "stay in our place," to keep our ambitions and joys within socially acceptable limits. Gradually, we internalize these limitations, accepting them as truths about what we deserve or what we are capable of achieving.

This conditioning creates mental boundaries, telling us how far we can go, how happy we can be, and how much we are allowed to desire from life. We carry these limits into adulthood, permitting ourselves only a narrow slice of fulfillment—not because that's all that's available, but because it's all we believe we deserve.

But what if, like the elephant, we are far more powerful than we think we are? What if the chains that bind us are illusions—mental constructs that dissolve if only we dare to question them? To transcend these confines, we must become fully present. In presence, we see clearly. The stories of the past and fears of the future fall away, and we realize that we are no longer confined. In this moment, we understand that our true potential for happiness, fulfillment, and success is vast and unlimited, waiting only for us to claim it.

To escape mental confines is to awaken to the truth that freedom is our natural state. We are unbound, unchained, and capable of extraordinary growth and joy. The limits we perceive are often nothing more than old stories, beliefs that we have the power to rewrite. When we become present, we remember that we are not small or limited, but powerful creators with the capacity for boundless expansion.

So dare to test the mental chains, to step beyond the limits you once accepted. Look at each belief, each boundary, and ask if it truly serves you. With each courageous step, each act of presence, you dismantle the invisible prisons of the mind and move closer to the freedom and joy that have been waiting for you all along.

THE REWARDS OF BEING YOURSELF

When we finally release the exhausting effort of maintaining facades and pretenses, something remarkable happens. The energy we once spent on performing becomes available for genuine creation and connection. This transformation is not merely a personal relief—it ripples outward, touching every aspect of our lives and leadership.

When we embrace our authentic nature, leadership becomes as natural as breathing, rather than feeling like a role we must constantly struggle to play. We no longer need to remember how we're "supposed" to act or second-guess our instincts. Instead, we respond to situations with an innate wisdom that arises from our ground of being. This authentic presence carries a natural authority that is far more powerful than any constructed leadership persona.

Our relationships deepen and become more meaningful when we show up as ourselves. The vulnerability of authentic self-expression creates a magnetic field that draws others into genuine connection. Team members sense they can trust us because we're no longer hiding behind a professional mask. This trust catalyzes more open communication, greater innovation, and stronger collaboration. Even challenging conversations become easier because they're grounded in truth rather than diplomacy.

Creativity flows more freely when we're being ourselves. When we stop filtering our ideas through the lens of what others might think or what's expected, we access a wellspring of original thinking. Solutions emerge more readily because we're no longer limiting our thinking to conventional approaches. Our unique perspective, shaped by our individual experiences and insights, becomes a valuable asset rather than something to suppress.

Perhaps most surprisingly, our energy increases dramatically when we stop performing. The constant drain of maintaining an image—monitoring ourselves, adjusting our behavior, checking others' reactions—falls away. In its place, we discover a natural vitality that comes from being aligned with our true nature. This isn't just physical energy; it's emotional and spiritual energy as well. We become more resilient in the face of challenges and recover more quickly from setbacks.

Decision making becomes clearer when we're anchored in our authentic self. Rather than weighing multiple perspectives on what we "should" do, we can tune into our inner wisdom and values. This doesn't mean decisions are always easy, but they become cleaner—less affected by external expectations and fears. We learn to trust our instincts while remaining open to input from others, finding a healthy balance between confidence and humility.

Our impact becomes more profound when we are ourselves. Paradoxically, the less we focus on "making an impact," the more influence we tend to have. People are drawn to authenticity in a world full of carefully curated images. When we model the courage to be ourselves, we give others permission to do the same. The resulting wave of authenticity can transform entire organizations.

Our relationship with power transforms, too. Instead of seeking power over others or trying to prove our worth, we begin to access Shakti—the natural power that flows through us when we're aligned with our true nature. This power is not about domination or control, but about becoming a clear channel for the creative force that wants to move through us in service of something larger than ourselves.

Even failure takes on a new meaning when we're being authentic. We no longer experience failure as a threat to our identity, but as feedback on our path of growth. It still hurts, but the pain is clean, free from the added layers of shame about not living up to an idealized image of who we think we should be.

Joy also becomes more accessible—not the fleeting happiness that comes from external validation, but a deeper contentment that arises from being in harmony with our true nature. We begin to experience ananda, or bliss—the natural state of our being when we're no longer fighting against ourselves or trying to be something we're not.

Perhaps most importantly, we discover that we already have everything we need. The constant seeking for validation, recognition, or completion subsides as we realize that our authentic self is already whole. This doesn't mean we become passive—quite the opposite. We engage more fully in life and leadership, but now we are acting from a place of sufficiency rather than lack.

This journey of authentic self-expression becomes both our path and our practice. Each moment offers a fresh invitation to choose presence over performance, truth over pretense, being over doing. And the more we accept these invitations, the more we discover that being ourselves is not just a possibility—it's the gateway to our highest contribution as leaders and as human beings.

CONSCIOUS LEADERS SPEAK
Be Yourself

Being yourself is not merely a personal goal—it is a sacred imperative for conscious leadership. Yet in a world that rewards conformity, performance, and posturing, this can be a revolutionary act. For the leaders we interviewed, authenticity has come through different portals: early grounding, cultural defiance, burnout, spiritual insight, or deliberate practice. Yet all of them agree: To lead from your soul, you must have the courage to stand in your truth.

Kip Tindell, cofounder of The Container Store, has long exemplified the ease that comes from inner congruence, modeling consistency without pretense. His natural transparency is a reminder that authenticity becomes a gift to others when you no longer feel the need to perform. "I don't have any trouble being myself. I've always been that way. Whether I'm with Joe Biden or a waiter at a restaurant, I'm just Kip. I think life's too short to be opaque. I want to be around people who are transparent—who aren't bogged down in deep-seated insecurities. Being yourself becomes easier when you're far enough along Maslow's hierarchy to not need to posture or pretend."[4]

Whole Foods Market cofounder John Mackey has always been outspoken, but his authenticity has matured and been tempered with age. "Being myself has never been hard—I've always been true to who I am. But that used to mean being blunt, opinionated, sometimes even insensitive. Over time, I've softened. I listen more. I speak with more compassion. I'm becoming more peaceful, more loving, more grounded. Authenticity isn't static—it's about who you're becoming."

For Gervase Warner, former CEO of the Massy Group, being himself meant dropping the Type A mask that had served him, but no longer fit. "For much of my professional life, I wore a mask: hard-charging, competitive, high-performing. And it worked—I thrived. But it wasn't the whole truth of who I am. In 2018, I decided: From here on, I'm going to lead from who I really am. I love people. I lead with empathy. I no longer want to play political games. I want to show up as my full self."

Mexican entrepreneur Marisa Lazo discovered that withholding emotion was costing her energy and connection. "For two years, I tried not to cry at work—because I thought strong leaders don't cry. But it didn't feel right. I realized I was more focused on not crying than on the message I was delivering. So I stopped pretending. I said, 'This is me. I cry when I'm moved.' That changed everything. My leadership deepened, my energy increased, and people felt more connected to me. I have learned that if you lead from your soul, you don't get tired. If you lead from a mask, you burn out."

WIN founder Kristin Engvig had to learn to claim her voice in a culture that prized conformity. "For a long time, I said, 'At WIN, we believe . . . .' I never said, 'I believe.' It felt like too much. Like I was showing off. But I had to heal that. I had to reclaim my voice. Now I say: 'I believe. I choose. I feel.' In Norway, standing out is scary. There's a strong current of 'don't shine too brightly.' But I remembered: We're not all meant to be the same. I had to be me."

Author and thought leader Avivah Wittenberg-Cox lives her authenticity through radical integration of roles, stages, emotions, and domains. "The corporate world loves to separate the personal from the professional. But I've never thought that way. Through my writing—especially my Elderberries blog—I connect all of it: work, family, dog, kids, aging, emotions. It's all one life. Why pretend otherwise?"

Simon Cohen, a former elite athlete and now CEO, discovered that being yourself isn't about rigidity—it's about resonance. "Being yourself doesn't mean being the same everywhere. You're not one fixed identity. You're a husband, a CEO, a son, a dreamer. I used to think consistency meant integrity. But now I know: I can be many things, and still be fully me. Different situations bring out different facets—not false masks, but facets, like a diamond. It's all me. Authenticity is about being true in the moment. Sometimes that truth is strength. Sometimes it's silence. But it's always honest."

Philosopher and management thought leader Ed Freeman reminds us that authenticity is not a personality trait, but an ongoing intention—a practice, not a posture. "Living authentically means trying to integrate all the parts of who you are. It's not something you arrive at—it's a human, fraught, lifelong effort. You fail, you fall short, you try again. But you keep trying to live with integrity, to live a life that makes sense to you and to those you care about."

For Doug Rauch, former president of Trader Joe's and former CEO of Conscious Capitalism Inc., authenticity is a discipline as well as an ethical obligation—one made possible by inner alignment. "There's always a cost to not being yourself. Maybe not right away, but over time, it shows up. Being yourself is a moral imperative. It means standing your ground when it matters, speaking up when something is wrong, and aligning who you are with how you live." Doug sees deep connectivity between the first three steps. "Self-love enables authenticity. When your worth comes from within, you're more likely to stand in your truth. These steps are connected—self-awareness, self-love, and self-expression are different facets of the same diamond."

Former professional athlete and FC Mother cofounder Morad Fareed's reclamation of self came through simplification—clearing away the clutter of people, roles, and performance. "It started with asking: Who do I enjoy being around? What kinds of conversations do I love? I cleaned the field—physically, emotionally, socially. I stopped intellectualizing. I followed my intuition. Now, I stay light. I avoid confrontational people. I don't need the noise. I want to uplift, to laugh, to be still. I want joy. I want to be me."

For Conscious Capitalism Inc. CEO Timothy Henry, being yourself requires deliberate spiritual practice and purpose alignment. "Authentic leadership means knowing your strengths, owning your shadows, and surrounding yourself with people who complement you. That's how you stay true. So much of my daily practice—meditation, journaling—is about preparing to be myself. Letting go of ego. Releasing attachment. Allowing my inner being to show up. Being yourself means living your values, even when it's inconvenient. When I became CEO of Conscious Capitalism Inc., it wasn't the most lucrative path—but it was the most aligned."

Each of these leaders embodies a different expression of authenticity—some fiery, some soft; some inherited, others hard-earned. But they all share one truth: Being yourself is not an indulgence; it is our responsibility. It is what makes conscious leadership real—and sustainable.

This chapter has highlighted the profound power of embracing your authentic nature, standing firmly in your values, and breaking free from the mental confines that have held you back. Being yourself means honoring your true essence and letting go of societal expectations and limitations so you can step into life fully, with courage and openness. This authenticity becomes the foundation for making strong, clear decisions.

The next step in the journey of self-discovery is to actively *choose* yourself—affirming your commitment to your path and your life. This means embracing not only who you are today but every part of your story, past and present, while consciously shaping the future you want to create.

CHAPTER 5

Choose Your Self

Just because I didn't choose my life doesn't mean I can't take ownership of it. Just because I didn't choose my life doesn't mean I can't choose to choose it.

—ANDRE AGASSI

What does it mean to *choose* yourself? It means choosing your past, your present, and your future. Choosing yourself goes beyond acceptance; it's about taking ownership of the events of your life and the decisions you've made along the way.

While knowing, loving, and being yourself lay the foundation, transformation truly begins when you actively choose how to show up in the world. This chapter will guide you toward recognizing your power to make conscious choices, enabling you to live without regrets, with gratitude, and with a strong sense of agency over your future.

We've deliberately used the word *choose* rather than *accept* or *create* because it emphasizes agency—the intentional act of embracing your life rather than reacting to it.

Betty Sue Flowers is an American poet, editor, and educator best known for her work at the intersection of literature, myth, leadership, and systems thinking. She played a pivotal role in bringing the insights of Joseph Campbell to a broader audience, most notably as the editor of *The Power of Myth*—the seminal book based on the celebrated 1988 PBS television series of the same name. She also served as editor for Joseph Jaworski's remarkable book *Synchronicity*. In our conversation, Betty Sue told us that choosing your life—even the painful parts—transforms fate into destiny:

> *We all begin with fate. Our family, our body, our upbringing, our place in time—these aren't things we choose. But at some point, when we say, "I choose this," even retroactively, fate becomes destiny. It's the act of claiming our life as our own that transforms it. It's no longer something that happened to us; it's something we're using to grow. We stop being victims. We become authors.*
>
> *Choosing yourself doesn't mean choosing what's easy. It often means choosing the very parts you once wished away—the difficult childhood, the heartbreak, the loss. But when you look back and say, "I choose to see this as part of my becoming," you transform pain into meaning, and meaning into joy. You're no longer a character in someone else's script. You're the protagonist. You're the hero. Choosing yourself is thus an act of agency. It's the moment you say, "This is my life. I accept all its gifts—even the painful ones." And in that choice, your story changes. Suffering becomes insight. Randomness becomes purpose. Fate becomes freedom.*

Of course, you can't choose what you don't yet know. We can't fully choose ourselves until we've already experienced life—and yet, we must choose in order to grow. This leads to a mysterious but generative loop: choosing reveals what was hidden, and revealing deepens choosing. As Betty Sue Flowers puts it:

> *You don't choose yourself in advance. That's the paradox. You can't—because you don't yet know who you are. You only begin to know through living—by responding, growing, stumbling, discovering. And then, with time and perspective, you look back and say, "Ah, this is who I am. And yes, I choose this." There's something mysterious about it. It's almost like a Möbius strip—you discover through living, and then you choose what you've discovered. And that choice deepens the discovery. You wouldn't have chosen it at the beginning—you didn't know what*

was in the package. But once you've lived into it, you begin to see the beauty. Choosing what you've been given—that's where the power is.

Choosing yourself is the antidote to shaping yourself to fit others' expectations. It's the foundation of genuine belonging. In the age of social media, we're trained to fit in. Young people are taught to edit themselves, filter themselves, shape their identities to match someone else's frame. But choosing yourself is the opposite. It's not about contorting to fit—it's about standing in your truth and saying, "This is who I am, and I claim it."

As Neha Sangwan says, the opposite of belonging isn't rejection—it's fitting in. You lose your soul when you abandon yourself in order to be accepted. Real belonging comes when you choose yourself fully—without shrinking or disguising who you are to make others comfortable.

CHOOSE YOUR PAST

The idea of choosing your past came to Raj one lunchtime, while he was at a silent retreat at Peace Village in Upstate New York. Volunteers stood behind the counter, serving food to each person in line. Since all communication with others was forbidden, there were no words, no gestures, no choices—you took what you were given.

As he sat down to eat, it struck Raj that this was an apt metaphor for life. Life isn't a buffet. Nor is there a menu to order from. You can't request more of this, less of that, or reject what seems unpalatable. You don't get to say, "I want this kind of mother, that kind of father, this religion, that socioeconomic status, this moment in history." Life hands you a tray—some of it bitter, some grossly unappetizing. But every morsel is necessary. It's all essential to your growth—to you becoming who you are meant to become.

Viewing it this way shifts your perspective on life. You step out of the shadow of victimhood if your path has been hard, or complacency if it's been easy. For decades, Raj saw himself as a victim of his own life, silently asking, "Why couldn't my father be like my friends' fathers—loving and kind? Why did I have to grow up in a family steeped in feudal values and misogyny?"

We've all had moments of looking back and thinking, "Why me?" But those difficult circumstances were often the exact fires we needed to walk through. Without experiencing the harshness of the patriarchal, feudal culture he was born into, Raj might never have developed the insight or depth to coauthor (with Nilima) *Shakti Leadership*, a book about the feminine, decades later.

When we look at our lives in this way, we start to see how the scattered pieces form a coherent narrative. Trust that even the parts you don't fully understand yet will make sense in time. Life isn't random; it's woven with meaning, if we choose to see it.

When we consciously choose to see our past as purposeful—even if we would never have chosen it in advance—it opens a narrative of growth and coherence. Social science research shows how framing your life as a heroic journey increases the experience of meaningfulness. As Betty Sue Flowers told us:

> *You don't always choose what happens to you—but you can choose the story you tell about it. We're often handed experiences long before we understand their meaning. But the moment you say, "I choose this," even retroactively, something shifts. Hardship becomes gift. That's why I love the word choose. It's not passive. It's an active verb. It doesn't deny pain; it transforms it. When you choose your life—fully and consciously—you step into a much larger narrative. You're no longer just the subject of fate. You become the cocreator of your story.*

You might say, "This is just a way to trick the mind"—and maybe it is. But perception shapes reality. We can view life through a lens of nihilism and declare that nothing matters, or we can choose to see life as a profound mystery that unfolds in a meaningful way to guide us toward our destiny.

Think of an experience in your life that was so painful, you'd never wish it on anyone. Now say to yourself, "I choose this." Feel how empowering that simple shift can be. You can't rewrite your past, but you can choose to embrace it. And in choosing it, you transform it into something that serves you rather than constrains you. This choice lifts you from the role of victim to one of quiet mastery. It shifts your mental state from agitation to equanimity.

In *Man's Search for Meaning*, Viktor Frankl wrote, "Everything can be taken from a man but one thing: the last of the human freedoms—to choose one's attitude in any given set of circumstances, to choose one's own way." We *can* find meaning in our suffering. Often, it inspires us to work to lessen that kind of suffering for others. The mother in Minnesota who started Mothers Against Drunk Driving (MADD) after her daughter was killed by a drunk driver illustrates this avenue of finding meaning in suffering.

Raj used this process to help reframe his relationship with his son:

> *My son, Alok, now thirty-six, was diagnosed as "special needs" at five. Before that, I delighted in him, with slight concern for traits that seemed different. Post-diagnosis, disappointment took hold—he wouldn't experience the life milestones we dream of for our children: college, independence, marriage. I began to see him as a burden, a lifelong responsibility that dulled the joy of fatherhood. But now, I say, "I choose him." This choice has made me a more patient, loving father, allowing me to see his beauty and his wisdom—not just his challenges. It has deepened my empathy and expanded my heart, impacting all aspects of my life.*

These lessons are not easy. Life can feel relentless and overwhelming. But beneath the hardship lies gold, waiting to be uncovered if we are willing to look with the right eyes. As Thich Nhat Hanh said, "No mud, no lotus."[1] The lotus flower of awakening blooms only through the mud of suffering.

The renowned Indian screenwriter and poet Javed Akhtar shares his wisdom on the beauty of accepting all of life's gifts: "What befalls everyone fell on me too. This was our share of bruises and blows. These bruises and blows did not go to waste. They came in handy. Had these trials not happened, many highlights of our lives would not have happened either. So this is the package. Accept it."[2]

Good Thing, Bad Thing, Who Knows?

This is a classic parable (often attributed to either Taoist or Sufi traditions) about the unpredictability of life. In a small, remote village, an old man and his son struggled to make ends meet. One day, the old man borrowed money from a lender to buy a magnificent stallion, hoping to breed it and secure his family's future. When he brought the horse back to the village, the townspeople gathered in awe, exclaiming, "You're going to be so wealthy! This is the best thing that could happen to you!" The old man simply replied, "Good thing, bad thing, who knows?" The villagers laughed, thinking him foolish.

By the next morning, the stallion had broken through the fence and disappeared. The villagers came running, exclaiming, "You're ruined! How will you ever repay the loan?" The old man replied with the same calm, "Good thing, bad thing, who knows?" The villagers thought he had lost his mind.

Days later, the stallion returned, this time with a herd of wild horses following him. The old man and his son now had more horses than they could have imagined. "It's a miracle!" the villagers cried, "You're going to be rich!" Yet again, the old man said, "Good thing, bad thing, who knows?"

While they were building a stronger fence to secure the horses, the stallion kicked the man's son and broke his leg, leaving him crippled. The villagers lamented, "This is terrible! No one will marry your son now. Your family line ends here." Once more, the old man replied, "Good thing, bad thing, who knows?"

Months later, the king declared war, drafting every able-bodied young man into the army. The old man's son, unable to serve due to his injury, was spared. Many of the village's young men perished in the war. The villagers now envied the old man. "You're so lucky," they said. "Your son is still with you." To which the old man responded, "Good thing, bad thing, who knows?"

The lesson is simple and profound: We can't ever know in the moment whether an event is truly good or bad. Each experience brings its own lessons and opportunities for growth, often hidden until we're ready to see them. Embrace what life brings without rushing to judgment, and see how you can grow from it.

Step out of the Drama Triangle

Drama often begins the moment another person enters your space. Alone, you may feel at peace, grounded in your own energy. But when a spouse, parent, or child steps into your field, harmony can quickly dissolve. The intersection of energies can create interference, disrupt your inner calm, and trigger dissonance. It's a universal experience—whether at home or work, moments of conflict are unavoidable. How we interpret and respond to them determines whether they become opportunities for growth or cause suffering.

Psychologist Stephen Karpman's *Drama Triangle* helps us understand these dynamics.[3] According to Karpman, in every conflict-ridden interaction, three roles emerge: the victim, the persecutor, and the rescuer. It usually begins with someone feeling victimized. The persecutor—a boss, partner, or family member—is labeled the "villain." The victim feels powerless and mistreated. The rescuer then steps in to help, seeking validation through being needed. This forms a cycle where the victim finds comfort in being saved, and the rescuer finds purpose in saving. For a time, the system holds an uneasy equilibrium.

But these roles are neither authentic nor conscious. They are ego-driven performances that inevitably unravel. The rescuer soon becomes drained, feeling as though their efforts are swallowed into a void. They begin to feel like a victim, and the original victim starts looking like a persecutor. The new "victim" may then start sympathizing with the original "villain" and look upon them as a rescuer. The cycle continues—a dance of emotional "musical chairs" with no resolution in sight.

The way out of the Drama Triangle is through a powerful reframing created by the late David Emerald, called the Empowerment Triangle.[4] In our book *Shakti Leadership*, Nilima refers to it as the Dharma Triangle. *Dharma*, rooted in Sanskrit, speaks to truth and righteous action. As shown in Figure 5, this transforms the Drama Triangle's limiting roles into empowering ones: Here, the victim sees themselves as a creator, reclaiming their power by asking, "How can I shape the outcome I want in this situation?" This shift replaces helplessness with agency and possibility.

The persecutor is now seen as a challenger—not as a threat but as a catalyst for self-mastery. The rescuer takes on the role of a coach. A good coach guides; they help you recognize your strength, encourage resilience, and support growth without fostering dependency.

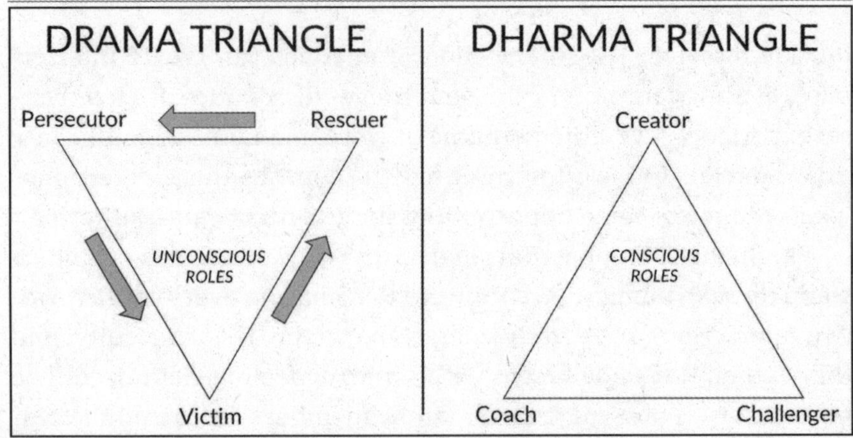

FIGURE 5. Drama Triangle versus Dharma Triangle. Used with permission from Stephen Karpman, and with thanks to David Emerald.

They stand beside you, asking penetrating questions rather than feeding you pat answers.

When we step consciously into these roles, we transform our interactions. The creator owns their path, the challenger pushes them to excel, and the coach offers insight and support. No longer caught in a cycle of blame and exhaustion, the roles align to elevate everyone involved.

Raj witnessed this transformation in his own family:

> *My brother lived in our parents' home, where my father held dominion. Steeped in a patriarchal mindset, our father tried to control many aspects of my brother's life, dictating even my sister-in-law's attire. Every time I visited, each cast himself as the victim and the other as the persecutor, pleading with me to "make Papa/Sanjay understand." Eventually, I chose to stop playing the rescuer. I told my brother, "Decide what will work for you and make that happen." He and his wife did just that, setting up a separate kitchen and living space within the house. This shift empowered them to engage with our father from a place of independence rather than forced dependency, creating some distance and gradually evolving their relationship to one of mutual and chosen interdependence.*

The Dharma Triangle shows us that by reframing difficult situations, we unlock new possibilities. Shifting our mindset from limitation to potential allows us to choose our responses, explore creative solutions, and approach challenges constructively.

HEALING LEADERS PRACTICE
Step into the Dharma Triangle

Think of a current situation where you feel wronged or powerless. Who is your persecutor? Who is showing up as a rescuer? How can you shift into a creative position to regain your power?

Keep in mind that you can be your own coach and your own challenger. This is a conscious way to create the reality you want without waiting for someone else to initiate the process.

HEALING LEADERS PRACTICE
Affirmation

I choose and embrace my past.

I choose all the people in my life, past and present.

I choose my parents, my grandparents, my siblings, my uncles and aunts, my cousins, my partner, my children, my friends, my colleagues, my leaders, my teachers, my supposed enemies, and everyone else who comes into my life.

I choose all the experiences I have enjoyed or endured, positive or negative.

I release all bitterness, anger, and regrets about my life. I am grateful for it all, and I choose it all.

CHOOSE YOUR PRESENT: LIVE IN GRATITUDE

Living in gratitude transforms how we experience life on a profound level. Gratitude shifts our focus from what we lack to what we have, opening us up to the abundance in our lives. When we consciously practice gratitude, it becomes a way of seeing—a lens through which we perceive the world and, ultimately, ourselves.

At its core, gratitude reminds us of our interconnection with others and the world. By acknowledging the gifts, kindness, and beauty surrounding us, we cultivate humility and respect, recognizing that much of what we value in life comes from beyond ourselves. This fosters empathy, patience, and a deeper sense of belonging and purpose.

Gratitude also profoundly impacts our mental and physical well-being. It can reduce stress, improve sleep, and strengthen the immune system. It helps us cope with adversity and bounce back from challenges by reinforcing resilience and hope. Gratitude even changes brain chemistry, releasing dopamine and serotonin—neurotransmitters that enhance mood and sustain a positive outlook.

Moreover, gratitude encourages us to live in the present, grounding us in the here and now. It reminds us that each moment, even those tinged with hardship, carries lessons and beauty. In this way, gratitude can transform our lives, turning even the simplest things—a warm meal, a kind word, a moment of quiet—into sources of joy and meaning.

Ultimately, gratitude elevates our consciousness. It brings us closer to a life of purpose, compassion, and harmony, enabling us to navigate life with greater appreciation, wisdom, and peace.

HEALING LEADERS PRACTICE
The Miracle of Life Visualization[5]

The following visualization is a powerful way to cultivate deep gratitude for the many aspects of life that we take for granted.

Close your eyes. Take a few deep, slow breaths and relax completely. You are about to embark on a profound journey: a journey to rediscover

the true miracle of life, to awaken to the extraordinary gifts that surround you in every moment—gifts you may never have truly seen or acknowledged.

In this visualization, we will begin by stripping away everything that you have not personally created and everything that you have taken for granted. We will then remove from your life everything that you have not "earned," yet feel entitled to. One by one, we will take away the many miracles of life that you have forgotten to appreciate.

Start with your body. Imagine that you can no longer walk. Your legs, once so capable, are now useless. Feel what it is like to lose the ability to move freely, to roam the earth on your own. Now, imagine that you have lost the power of speech. Words, conversations, laughter—gone. Now, you can no longer smell. The fragrances of flowers, food, even fresh air all vanish.

Now imagine you cannot see. Darkness envelopes you. All the vibrant colors, the faces of loved ones, the enormous beauty of the world, are erased from your life. Your sense of taste disappears—you can no longer take pleasure in food or drink. You reach out to touch something, but there is no sensation, no feeling in your fingertips. You cannot hear music, laughter, or even the comforting sound of another human voice. You are enveloped in overwhelming silence.

But it doesn't stop there. The world around you changes too. You have no home—no walls to shelter you, no cozy space to return to. All the beauty around you is gone. There are no trees, no flowers, no rivers, no lakes. The sky has emptied of clouds, the rain has vanished, the warmth of the sun no longer touches you. The seasons themselves have disappeared—no more spring blossoms, no golden autumn leaves.

Transportation has ceased. No cars, no planes, no trains—no way to move through the world. And the animals—all of them—have disappeared. There are no birds in the sky, no dogs, no cats, no other creatures sharing this earth with you. Plants are gone too. Food now comes in the form of a tasteless pill—no water, no flavors, no nourishment from the earth.

All the marvelous technologies that you use every day and have come to take for granted are gone. No computers, no smartphones, no internet, no large-screen televisions.

Perhaps the most profound loss of all: There are no relationships. You are utterly alone. No mother, no father, no children, no friends. No one to love or be loved by. You exist in isolation, aware that others are out there but unable to see them, touch them, or connect with them in any way whatsoever.

Pause here. Stay in this world for a moment—this cold, empty, silent world without sensation, without beauty, without love.

Pause.

Now . . . let us begin again.

First, let there be light. Feel your eyes heal as you open them to the world once more. Colors flood back into your life—brilliant, radiant, alive. You can see the faces of your loved ones again, their smiles, their eyes shining with emotion.

Your ears open up, and the sounds of life return—the laughter of friends, the songs of birds, the rustle of leaves in the wind. You can speak again, share your thoughts, your love, your gratitude. Your legs regain their strength. Feel the joy of movement, of walking through the world with ease and grace.

Now, your sense of touch is restored. You can feel the softness of a loved one's embrace, the warmth of the sun on your skin, the cool breeze on your face. Taste returns. Savor the sweetness of a ripe mango, the richness of a hot cup of coffee, the joy of savoring your favorite foods once again.

Look around—trees have returned in their splendor, filling the world with vibrant greens, golds, and reds. Flowers bloom, their beauty overwhelming your senses. The rivers flow once more, and the majestic mountains rise to meet the sky. The seas stretch out endlessly, their waves bringing peace to your soul.

The sky is full again—clouds, rain, snow, the warmth of the sun, the glow of the moon, and the countless stars lighting up the night. The seasons are back, each with its own unique beauty. All the animals—the dogs, the cats, the birds—have returned, filling the earth with life and companionship.

All the conveniences of modern life are yours again: hot showers, clean water, the internet, smartphones, computers, airplanes, cars—all the inventions that make life so much easier, so much more connected.

And now, relationships flood back into your life. You are surrounded by people who love you—family, friends, loved ones. You can hold them, laugh with them, cry with them. You can share in the joy of being deeply connected to others, of loving and being loved.

All of this—every bit of it—is a gift. None of it was earned by you. It was all given to you freely, yet you had become indifferent to the miracle of it all.

Take a moment to feel the immensity of this realization. Breathe it in. You are surrounded by miracles, every single day. And now, you know what it would be like to lose it all.

But you haven't lost it. It's still here. It's all here, right in front of you.

Open your eyes. Look around. Feel the leaf or flower in your hand,[6] the ground beneath your feet, the breath in your lungs.

This is the miracle of life.

Do not take it for granted. Commit to living from this day forward in a state of deep, profound gratitude for every precious moment, for every gift you have been given. Hold onto this feeling, carry it with you, and let this awareness change the way you see the world—forever.

CHOOSE YOUR FUTURE: EMBRACE THE HEROIC JOURNEY

The hero's journey, as defined by Joseph Campbell, is a powerful way to understand our lives and how we are meant to grow.[7] To become who we are meant to be, we each must undertake a heroic journey. A universal narrative pattern found in myths and stories across cultures, this journey symbolizes personal growth, self-discovery, and integration. It reflects an inner journey as much as an outer one, offering a timeless framework for human transformation and the pursuit of meaning.

Let's explore the key dimensions and applications of this profound work—insights that are especially powerful for leaders.

The Heroic Journey Summarized

When Campbell identified the universal pattern of the heroic journey across time and cultures, he mapped it into seventeen stages.

Later, Christopher Vogler adapted it for screenwriting, refining it to twelve stages.[8] To keep it simple, we've distilled it further into a four-stage model, illustrated in Figure 6.

The journey begins with a crisis—a life-shaking event that disrupts the hero's (or heroine's) ordinary existence. They receive a call to adventure and must leave the familiar world behind. This call pulls them into an unknown realm filled with challenges and even trauma.

As you navigate this new reality, you must confront your deepest fear. In this defining moment, it's you against your shadow, facing what terrifies you most. The journey carries danger but is also key to growth and maturation. You face trials, gain allies, confront your greatest fear, and achieve a decisive victory. To paraphrase Joseph Campbell, "The cave you fear to enter contains the treasure you seek." There's no way around it—the only path is through. Your old self must die so that you

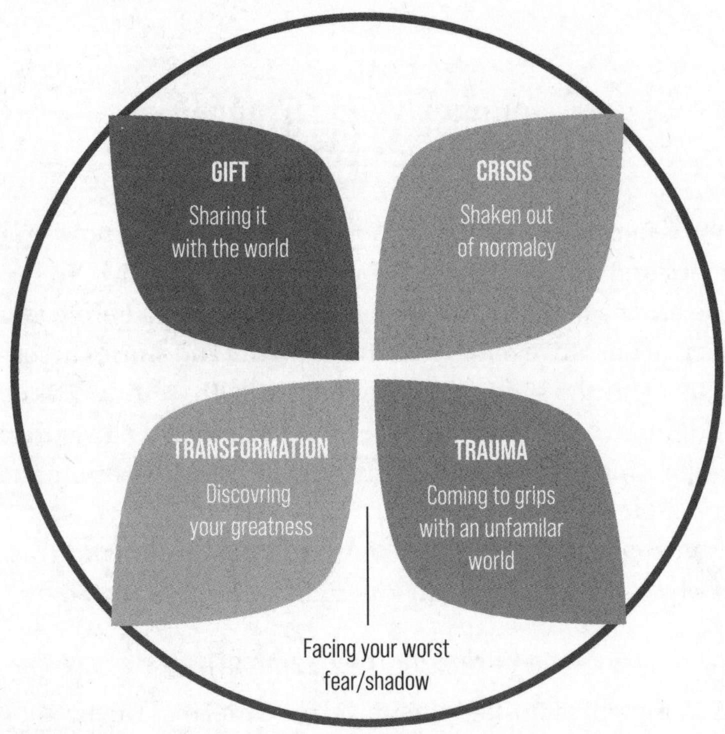

FIGURE 6. The Four-Stage Heroic Journey

can be reborn as a more potent being, much like a caterpillar transforming into a butterfly. In facing your fears, you undergo profound personal growth. New capacities emerge, and latent powers come to light. Your inherent greatness, long dormant, awakens. This transformation brings newfound strength and resilience.

Following this, you return to the ordinary world, bringing newfound wisdom and an elixir back to your community. This gift is exactly what your "world"—your team, family, community, or organization—needs to move forward. Only by sharing what you've gained do you complete the heroic cycle.

The heroic journey teaches us that when we are faced with seemingly insurmountable challenges, we must first grow. Only by evolving to a new level can we rise to the task.

We represent this journey as a circle because it's cyclical. In life and leadership, we are called to undertake it repeatedly. Every crisis, large or small, invites a fresh adventure—a new heroic journey. Each time you confront a deep fear and emerge transformed, you discover hidden strengths and greatness within.

HEALING LEADERS PRACTICE
Remember an Ordeal You've Overcome

Use the following questions to make sense of how you successfully navigated a major challenge in your life, framing it as a heroic journey:

- **What was the crisis, and how were you shaken out of normalcy or your comfort zone?**
- **Did you heed the call, or refuse/resist? Why?**
- **How were you tested, and who were your allies and enemies?**
- **What was your greatest fear, and how did you overcome it?**
- **What new capacities did you gain, and how did you grow from the experience?**
- **How are you showing up differently now, as a person or a leader?**
- **What are you offering your world, and how has it changed for the better as a result?**

Nilima shares:

My first true heroic journey at work began in 1998, after I had spent a dazzling ten years in the corporate world, working with blue-chip companies like ITC-Sheraton, Philips, and ESPN STAR Sports. I had been the blue-eyed girl of every boss I worked with, effortlessly cruising from one creative success to the next in my chosen field of corporate communications and public relations.

In hindsight, the ten-year mark now stands out clearly as a classic "call to adventure," though I had no idea at the time. I was thirty-two and riding high on professional success. To celebrate, now that I was earning a comfortable living, I bought what I thought was a "smart" art investment—a beautiful Tibetan thangka (a meditative painting).

Almost overnight, my work life unraveled. That thangka became, quite unexpectedly, the symbolic herald that disrupted my comfort zone. Suddenly, I was plunged from the heights of success into a disorienting abyss where I felt I could do nothing right. From being seen as a rising star, I began to feel like a complete failure. This triggered a profound identity crisis. Every foundation I had relied on for my sense of self was called into question.

When my boss turned into my harshest critic, a colleague offered a lifeline: "Have you tried yoga? Its philosophy holds answers to the very questions you're asking—'Who am I?' and 'Why am I here?'" My greatest fear at that moment was being fired. But as fate would have it, my husband was transferred from Singapore to London, and this move became my portal to a new path. It felt like the invisible hand of the Guru appearing when the student is ready.

In yoga, I found myself again—on a much deeper level. I had "arrived" at a path I have not left since. It became the foundation for my transformation into a spiritual guide and integral health practitioner. The two books I've written so far—and now this one—are the elixirs I've returned with, offerings born from my own descent, death, and resurrection through the heroic journey of conscious leadership.

Journeying Consciously

Campbell's work suggests that the heroic journey usually begins with a crisis. But can we grow without crisis and suffering? Becoming aware of and reframing the elements of the journey allows us to experience growth in all circumstances with greater ease and grace. The *conscious* heroic journey—Nilima's original idea, first proposed in *Shakti Leadership*—unfolds through four stages: evolutionary impulse, followed by dissolution, evolution, and resolution (see Figure 7).

Let's explore each of these stages.

Evolutionary Impulse

The journey begins with an evolutionary impulse. Our planet was once only water and lava. Over eons, plants emerged. Then animals. Then humans. The Earth didn't decide to evolve; the vast intelligence of nature guided its growth. As human beings, we have the capacity to recognize this evolutionary impulse and ask, "Can I partner with it? Can I consciously evolve and participate in nature's unfolding?"

Within each of us lies our purpose, the meaning of our existence—a seed carrying its own evolutionary impulse. This innate

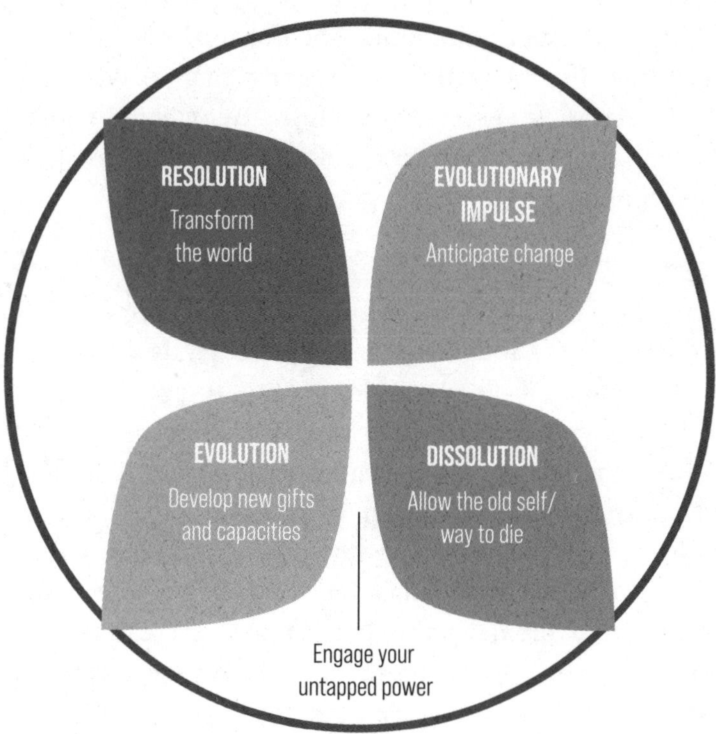

FIGURE 7. The Conscious Heroic Journey

drive awakens at pivotal moments, urging us toward growth. Too often, we ignore the call, allowing inertia, complacency, and conditioning to stifle it. But the truth remains: The entire universe is structured to evolve us, whether we cooperate or not. If we resist conscious evolution, life may bring a crisis to awaken us to our potential.

Dissolution

Every evolution requires a dissolution—a sacrifice or surrender. When you accept this willingly, you don't need to suffer pain or trauma. Dissolution is essential; only by disrupting the old order can a new, elevated one emerge.

As humans, we cling to life and resist the idea of death. Yet part of the journey is learning to let go of the fear associated with dying. Death is inseparable from life; it is woven into it. And it brings essential gifts.

Anticipate dissolution; let your old self, your old identity or old ways die, just as a caterpillar must "die" for the butterfly to emerge. This is a psychological death: a necessary letting-go. When we resist it, it often arrives as a painful breakdown. But when we embrace it, dissolution becomes transformation, releasing the energy waiting to be awakened.

Evolution

The evolution stage is where you step into your unrealized potential, unlocking dormant energy and capabilities. Imagine untapped reserves within you—like batteries waiting to be activated. You've drawn from one set; now you're ready to discover the next. This stage is about releasing that hidden energy, allowing it to flow freely and empower you to reach new heights.

Fresh gifts and capacities begin to emerge; you discover abilities you never knew you had. This is the birth of a new self, one with expanded vision, greater strength, and deeper creativity. Through this unfolding, you become more than you were, evolving toward a fuller expression of your highest potential.

Resolution

In the resolution stage, you return to your world to share your newly acquired gifts and put them to use to bring about fresh transformations—whether in your family, relationships, team, or organization. With these new capacities, you are prepared to meet challenges with wisdom, presence, and power.

Even at the journey's end, stay fully present and alive to the potential within each moment. Avoid slipping into autopilot, reacting unconsciously to life's churn. Recognize that you've just emerged from a cycle of growth and are in a moment of rest. But accept that this pause won't last forever—change will come again. When it does, embrace it by letting go of what no longer serves you and moving forward. Not every journey is life-altering; many small journeys occur between the larger ones, each adding layers of growth and new capacities. These smaller adventures equip you with the ability to bring resolution to any challenge you face.

HEALING LEADERS PRACTICE
Where Are You in Your Conscious Heroic Journey?

Use the following questions to assess where you are and what you can expect:

- **What stage are you at? Evolutionary impulse, dissolution, evolution, or resolution?**
- **Have you heeded the call? If not, why not?**
- **Have you explored the new world, with all its possibilities?**
- **What is your deepest fear? What inner demon do you need to slay?**
- **What is your unrealized potential (your gift/greatness)?**
- **When you find your elixir, how will you offer it to the world?**
- **As you explore these questions, what are you learning about yourself?**

The Only Way Out is In and Through

The central teaching of the heroic journey is to embrace each challenge as a call to adventure. Shift your mindset and set forth. Don't yield to fear or hesitation; view each obstacle as a gift—an opportunity to become a better version of yourself—and embrace it with gratitude.

True leadership requires the courage to journey inward and come fully into yourself. The only way out is in. No one else can walk this path for you. The power, the resources—everything you need for this journey—already lives within you. And once you commit, external allies will appear to support you along the way.

There are times when we choose to embark on a journey, and times when we don't. For every journey we take, there may be many we resist. What compels us to step forward in some cases, but not others?

Each of us may have a unique answer to that question. It could be fear, inertia, or a desire to preserve the comfort of the status quo. It might be a sense that we're not yet ready to confront a challenge that feels daunting. Or perhaps it's an instinctual sense that the timing isn't right—that such a test might be too much, risking our emotional or physical stability.

Eventually, however, a time will come—a pivotal choice-point, a moment of reckoning—when the journey can no longer be postponed. Not moving forward ceases to be an option; life demands it. And in that moment, the only way out is through.

Consider the heroic journey of the wildebeest, captured in many African nature documentaries. Each year, they must cross vast, crocodile-infested rivers. But the crocodiles do not deter the herd. There is no alternative; they plunge forward, and many perish. They go because they must. For the human soul, the journey is similar. When we arrive in this world, not living is not an option, and neither is not evolving along the way. We are called to grow, or we risk a kind of internal death.

CONSCIOUS LEADERS SPEAK
Choose Yourself

Our conversations with conscious leaders addressed how they came to claim, accept, and cocreate their lives with intention and courage. This entails the reframing of past stories, midlife choices and reinventions, and the deep spiritual authorship of one's life path. To choose yourself is to move from fate to freedom—not by denying your past, but by claiming authorship of your story. Conscious leaders know that we do not get to choose what happens to us. But we can choose how to respond, how to interpret, and how to grow. Choosing yourself is not a one-time act—it is a daily invitation to embrace your life as it is, while actively shaping what it can become. Here's how eleven leaders have walked that path.

For Avivah Wittenberg-Cox, choosing yourself begins by choosing the story you tell about your life. "Terrible things can and do happen. But if you reframe it—if you find meaning and growth in it—you elevate the experience itself. That's what I've always done through writing. It's how I metabolize and transform life."

Doug Rauch looks at this step through the lens of radical acceptance—choosing not just your path forward, but the full truth of your life. "I'd reframe this from 'choose' to 'accept.' And I don't mean resignation; I mean the honest acknowledgment of what is. Only when we fully accept the truth of our lives—past, present, all of it—can we make meaningful choices about who we want to become."

Ed Freeman urges us to move beyond passivity and into authorship—not just of the self, but of the life one chooses to live. "I prefer the phrase 'creating your life.' You're not just a character in your story; you're the author. It's not about following a script—it's about crafting something that makes sense to you and to the people you care about. You make decisions—some wise, some foolish—and those choices shape your canvas. Life becomes the art you're creating and living."

For Gervase Warner, choice showed up in a moment of loss. He had to embrace the closing of a chapter he didn't want to close to be able to move forward. "The hardest choice I had to make was choosing how I left Massy.

It was painful. It wasn't how I wanted the story to end. But eventually—especially during my Camino [de Santiago] walk—I stopped resisting. I accepted what had happened. And that was the real choice: to own my story, even the parts I wouldn't have picked for myself."

Kristin Engvig's life has been shaped by a series of courageous decisions, each one bringing her closer to alignment, growth, and impact. "The first big choice came when I had my son. I couldn't do everything anymore, so I professionalized WIN. It grew. The second was leaving my husband and a toxic relationship. That same year, WIN had its biggest event. It was like the universe said: Now you're in alignment. Later, I had to choose myself financially. I realized I hadn't saved enough. I had to say: I matter. My well-being matters. That was the hardest choice. But I keep making it—every day."

For Marisa Lazo, choosing herself came through pausing and reframing what she had once rejected. "As a teenager, I used to wish I had a different father—someone calmer, more 'normal.' But through meditation and therapy, I saw the gifts. Today, I wouldn't trade my father for anyone. I am who I am because of him. To choose yourself, you have to pause—not once, but regularly. That's how you reflect. That's how you integrate. That's how you live with intention."

Simon Cohen reframes choosing as falling in love—with your fate, with your story, with your imperfect self. "Choosing yourself means choosing to love what you've been given—even if it's not what you would've picked. It's like many arranged marriages. You grow into love. You fall in love with what's already yours. I didn't choose my family, my country, or the losses I've lived through. But I choose to embrace them. And if I look in the mirror and don't like what I see, I don't complain—I change. Not the nose or the eyes—but how I see myself. That's where the real power is."

Timothy Henry was handed a difficult beginning. But he now sees choosing himself as honoring his roots. "I use the word 'accept.' I can't redo my beginnings. But I can honor them. Even the hard parts. They gave me drive, empathy, and strength. Accepting that is how I move forward. The experiences I had—the foster care, the trauma—shaped the skills I needed to do this work. And I've come to appreciate even that. There's wisdom in the wound."

John Mackey sees choosing yourself as stepping fully into your cocreative power. "I believe I helped create my past through my previous karma.

And I'm creating my present and future through my actions. We're not victims—we're creators. Choosing yourself means claiming that authorship. You get to decide what story your life is telling. You get to interpret it in an empowering way."

Morad Fareed's turning point came when he stopped resisting pain and reframed it as part of a sacred curriculum. "The 'Why me?' mindset never ends. But you start to realize: The suffering isn't random. It's your training. It's preparing you for something sacred. We ask, 'Why me?' when bad things happen. We should also ask, 'Why me?' when we're blessed. Why were we chosen to receive the gifts we were given? That's part of choosing yourself—saying yes to the whole package."

Kip Tindell offers a grounded reminder that gratitude is not a reaction—it's a conscious decision. "I had a Leave It to Beaver childhood—very idyllic. But I don't take any of that for granted. I choose to live with gratitude every day. That's the key to happiness. Sure, there've been hard moments. Watching The Container Store struggle since I stepped away has been like watching your child go down a painful path. But I try not to get stuck in trauma. I stay conscious. I choose to be grateful. That has made all the difference."

Each of these leaders has chosen their life—not by erasing its hardships, but by stepping into authorship. They have rewritten their narratives, reframed their pain, reclaimed their voice, and reconnected with their power. They remind us: Choosing yourself is not selfish. It is the foundation for a life lived with purpose, impact, and joy.

In this chapter, you explored the profound act of choosing yourself—taking ownership of your life and making empowered decisions that align with your deepest truths. In the next chapter, you'll learn how to translate self-acceptance and conscious choice into action. This is where you choose growth over safety, taking the bold steps needed to learn and live your purpose. *Expressing* yourself means showing up in the world and sharing your gifts fully and joyfully.

CHAPTER 6

Express Your Self

Each seed has within it the potential to become a forest.
—BOB ANDERSON

As human beings, we are born with extraordinary untapped capacities and enormous potential. *Expressing* yourself is about moving toward the full realization of our boundless potential. How can we cast our light into the world, in all its brilliance and authenticity?

As Indian mystic Sadhguru says, most creatures on Earth exist within the constraints of instinct and biological programming. Animals are largely bound by the limitations of their physical and genetic design, following a predictable cycle of survival, reproduction, and death. They operate within what Sadhguru calls a "lower line" and an "upper line," meaning they are born with a fixed range of potential. An elephant can become a bigger, stronger elephant—but that's it.

Humans, however, are different. We do not have an upper line; we are born with unlimited potential, an unlimited capacity for growth, transformation, and self-realization. While our biological needs impose a "lower line" for survival, we possess consciousness, creativity, and the ability to choose. This enables us to grow intellectually, emotionally, and spiritually, to redefine what life means and live with a purpose far beyond mere survival.

With this freedom comes a profound responsibility. Without an upper boundary, we can strive to create extraordinary beauty, harmony, and consciousness in society—or cause terrible harm. Our choices shape our lives and the world around us. The path to meaningful fulfillment lies in recognizing this vast potential and choosing a life of awareness and purpose.

Nilima's beloved teacher college, Father Lancy, taught her that we should go through life with two pebbles in our pockets: one to remind us that we are nobody, and not to take ourselves too seriously, and the other to remind us that without us, the universe is incomplete. Until we fully become ourselves and express our full potential, the world remains unfinished. We should embrace this paradox, lightly and with responsibility.

Expressing yourself is not just a personal act; it is a sacred full obligation. When we hold back a part of ourselves, we deprive the world of something irreplaceable. Our stories, our voices, our insights—these are what shape the human experience and the experience of all life on the planet. Each of us has a role to play in the great symphony of life. When we rise to express ourselves fully, we add richness to the collective melody of humanity.

Imagine a world where every person feels empowered to bring forth their gifts. How much more beauty, how much more wisdom, how much more love would circulate through this world? By expressing yourself, you ignite a spark in others, inspiring them to step forward and do the same. You grant permission to those around you to find and share their voices too.

To express yourself is to claim your place in the world—to say, *I am here, and I have something to offer.* It is to step out from the shadows of self-imposed limitations, to hone and bring forth your unique gifts, and to change the world by your presence.

This is our invitation to you. Let your music flow. Speak your truth. Cast your light. The world is waiting for what only you can bring.

CHOOSE GROWTH OVER SAFETY

In life, we often face forks in the road—moments where we must choose between growth and safety. Will you stay on the familiar path, or you step through a newly opened door, uncertain of what lies beyond? Will you heed the call to evolve, expand, and experience the next chapter of your potential? Or will you remain where you're comfortable, doing what you already know, resting in the shelter of familiarity?

Every one of us faces this choice countless times. We can stay in the cozy cocoon of what we know, or listen to that inner call urging us to shed our skin, spread our wings, and embrace the unknown. This is the choice between living as a caterpillar or becoming a butterfly. But unlike the caterpillar, whose transformation is automatically guided by nature, we humans are tasked with consciously triggering our own growth. Philosopher Peter Koestenbaum put it beautifully: "We've reached such explosive levels of freedom that, for the first time in history, we have to manage our own mutation."[1] Nature won't step in and flip the switch for us. We have to locate the switch within ourselves and choose when and how we will evolve.

Opportunity knocks, but it never shoves. The decision to grow, transcend, and step into a larger version of ourselves is ours alone.

Raj shares how this has shown up in his life:

> *I've encountered the choice between growth and safety many times. One vivid instance was in 2013, when I was at Bentley University. Babson College approached me with a compelling offer: an endowed chair and a higher-profile platform to promote Conscious Capitalism. For years, I had made clear to the leadership at Bentley that I wanted to focus solely on teaching and writing about Conscious Capitalism, not continue to teach marketing. They had stonewalled, citing a lack of resources. When I informed Bentley's president of my planned departure, she said, "You are not going to Babson. Give me until the evening, and please do not sign anything!" Now that Babson had extended an offer, Bentley moved with alacrity. Sure enough, they put together a lucrative package and offered it to me that evening.*
>
> *I now faced a dilemma. Bentley's offer was considerably better financially, and it was the safe choice. I'd been there for fifteen years*

and knew the people, the rhythm, the culture. Moving to Babson would mean stepping into the unfamiliar and building a new community from scratch. But Babson was the world's leading school for entrepreneurship, and the synergy between Conscious Capitalism and entrepreneurship was profound. I reached out to John Mackey for advice. He asked me, "Which choice will help you grow more, rather than simply feel safe?" I felt my answer unfold. Making a decision solely based on money would be a betrayal of my beliefs. The path ahead was clear: I chose Babson, knowing it would challenge me and force me to grow. It would also take me further in fulfilling my purpose.

Years later, the opportunity to move from Babson to Tecnológico de Monterrey posed a similar challenge. This too required letting go of the known and embracing a new frontier, with its own set of risks and rewards. For one, it meant giving up academic tenure, the guarantee of lifetime employment. It also meant ten additional weeks of travel a year to Mexico. Once again, I chose growth over safety and decided to leave Babson. Tecnológico de Monterrey was deeply committed to Conscious Capitalism, and to establishing a new center to further teaching, research, and executive education in the field.

These choices are complex: Growth isn't always the right path, and safety can sometimes be the wiser option when it supports with stability and well-being. Not every risk is worth the reward. But if we choose growth more often than not, we begin to evolve into the people we are meant to be. Whatever path we take, it's essential that we make our choices consciously—not from fear, but in alignment with our values and purpose.

Financial considerations are often a factor in choosing the safe path. Pursuing your purpose may initially mean less material gain. But when you align with your purpose and let growth be your compass, abundance tends to follow—not only in terms of material prosperity, but also in the form of deep, lasting fulfillment.

FIND YOUR ZONE OF GENIUS

Consider what Gay Hendricks calls the "zone of genius." This concept is transformative, inviting us to examine how we operate in life and work and to consciously choose a path that lets our unique brilliance shine. In his book *The Big Leap*, Hendricks describes four zones of functioning, each representing different levels of potential, engagement, and fulfillment:

ZONE OF INCOMPETENCE

This zone includes all the tasks that simply aren't your strong suit—things you don't know how to do and have little interest in learning. Countless others can do these tasks better and faster than you. For instance, imagine a high-earning consultant, accustomed to billing $1,000 an hour, who spends half a Saturday struggling to connect a new printer to their computer. Instead of wasting those hours, they could have paid a tech-savvy teenager $50 to handle the job. In our specialized world, many tasks fall into this category. The lesson: Save your time, energy, and focus for what truly matters to you, and outsource what doesn't.

ZONE OF COMPETENCE

This zone includes tasks you know how to do well, and perhaps even enjoy to a degree, but that many others can do just as well. You're competent here, but not operating at your peak. Is taking on these tasks the best use of your valuable time? Could you be pursuing something greater instead? Letting go of this zone opens space for more meaningful work and growth.

ZONE OF EXCELLENCE

This is where many of us spend most of our time—and are tempted to stay. This zone includes things you do extremely well, perhaps even effortlessly. You're recognized, rewarded, and admired for this work. Yet, it's familiar territory that can grow stale over time. For an academic, it might mean teaching the same course for a decade; for a speaker, delivering the same talk year after year. It pays well and pleases others, but it no longer challenges or excites you.

ZONE OF GENIUS

Beyond excellence lies your zone of genius. This is where your unique gifts reside and extraordinary contributions emerge—ones that only you can make. Here you feel most alive, fulfilled, and connected to your purpose. The gravitational pull of the zone of excellence is strong, making it easy to settle there, seduced by comfort and reward. But the zone of genius calls you to step into something more—riskier, but potentially transformative. This is where you grow, stretch, and evolve, unlocking creativity, insight, and impact that are uniquely yours. The work here demands that you dig deep, becoming the fullest expression of your potential.

Finding your zone of genius often requires taking a heroic journey—a courageous step into the unknown. It asks you to choose growth over safety, to emerge from the comfortable cocoon and step into a life of perpetual evolution.

Stepping into your zone of genius doesn't mean abandoning everything else; your zone of excellence can remain a solid foundation. But the real magic happens when you challenge yourself to go beyond comfort, daring to explore, create, and inspire in ways only you can.

LIVE CONSCIOUSLY, NOT COMPULSIVELY

Most human actions stem from unconscious patterns, reactions, and habits, some of which can be described as compulsions. When we live compulsively, we're driven by habitual responses, cravings, fears, and desires that often lie below the surface of our awareness. We react automatically to situations rather than responding mindfully. Living compulsively means being enslaved by our own mind, body, and emotions, bound by old conditioning and unchecked urges.

In contrast, living consciously is about moving through life with deliberate awareness and intentionality. It involves cultivating a higher level of self-awareness, where we are fully present in each moment, able to observe our thoughts, emotions, and actions without being controlled by them. Living consciously is liberating because it allows us to harness our inner power, shape our lives intentionally, and live in alignment with our higher self.

At its core, living consciously entails self-mastery. The first step is learning to witness yourself—to observe your mind, body, and emotions without judgment. Through practices like meditation, mindfulness, and yoga, we can become more attuned to our internal states and thus gain greater control over our reactions. This awareness frees us from automatic behaviors and brings greater clarity to our decisions, enabling us to respond with wisdom rather than knee-jerk reactions.

Living consciously also involves releasing our attachment to the ego. Much of our compulsive behavior is rooted in ego-driven desires—our need for validation, power, material wealth, or external approval. When we live consciously, we transcend this small self.

Expressing yourself means living consciously, not compulsively. Conscious living is a path to freedom. It liberates us from the endless pursuit of compulsive desires, from a life of constant yearning, frustration, and emptiness. Living consciously means engaging fully in life without being consumed by it, recognizing that true happiness and meaning come from making conscious choices.

THE HEROIC JOURNEY LEADS TO PURPOSE

Every one of us will journey through multiple transformations in our lives, each offering us the choice to step into a deeper, truer version of ourselves.

Raj recalls:

> *I joined Bentley University in 1998. Bentley was positioning itself as the business school for the information age, creating endowed faculty positions that focused on the intersection of business and information technology. I was offered one of these positions: Trustee Professor of Marketing, a prestigious title accompanied by a 60 percent pay raise, half the normal teaching load, a research assistant, a travel budget, and all the trappings of status. I took the position enthusiastically, feeling I'd been handed a golden opportunity, and moved my family from Washington, DC to Boston. I bought a Mercedes and stretched my finances to buy an expensive house.*

At the time, teaching marketing was just a role I fulfilled. I was interested in information technology, but it was not a passion. I felt no deep connection to the work. For a while, I had some momentum in my new, high-profile role. I dreamed up the idea of creating a Center for Marketing Technology, in which the university promptly invested over a million dollars. Bentley asked me to run the center full-time. I didn't want to manage people or oversee budgets, but eventually I succumbed to pressure and agreed to do it. My heart was simply not in it, and my efforts dwindled. The center lay dormant, an expensive "white elephant."

Four years in, the university faced the decision of whether to renew my endowed professorship. This was usually a formality, but not in my case. Of the two trustee professorships, only one was renewed—and it wasn't mine. It was a public demotion, a humiliating stripping away of status and privilege. My teaching load doubled, my salary decreased, and my assistant and travel budget vanished. The impact was both professional and deeply personal. I fell into a depression, a dark period of self-doubt and isolation. I wrestled with feelings of shame and failure.

In that darkness, a quiet realization began to surface. "You were not fulfilled in that work," a voice within me whispered. "You never felt truly alive doing it." What began as a crisis soon revealed itself as an invitation to connect with what actually mattered to me. This was my opportunity to commit to work that held meaning, to teaching and writing about something that I deeply cared about. I made a solemn, internal promise to focus on what really mattered to me and to the world—work that would ignite my spirit and impact others.

I set concrete goals for myself, including winning Bentley's annual Teaching Award as well as the Scholar of the Year Award—not for the sake of recognition, but to prove to myself that I was capable of doing high-quality work of significance and value. Without fanfare, I began to delve into topics I truly cared about. One inquiry led to another, and soon I was on the path to writing Firms of Endearment*—a journey that would lead to the founding of the Conscious Capitalism movement and transform my life and the lives of countless others.*

Looking back, that crisis was a doorway. It was a painful but necessary disintegration of my old self, stripping away what no longer fit and making space for the work that would ultimately make a tangible difference in the world. Guides appeared along the way, as they often do on a heroic journey, illuminating the path forward and challenging me to grow into a new version of myself.

The work I did after that turning point was different. Now, everything felt aligned. My work began to resonate with others. I wasn't just creating content; I was contributing to a meaningful movement. My heart was fully engaged. Eventually, I did win those two awards I'd silently set as my goals. By then, they were simply symbols, reminders of a deeper truth: that this journey, this crisis, had been an initiation into my higher purpose.

We all face these moments. Life presents us with crises and crossroads, sometimes through failure, disappointment, or loss. In these dark days, we may feel as if we are unraveling, but in truth, we are being given the chance to shed the parts of ourselves that no longer serve us. In these moments, we are invited to embrace a higher calling, to let go of what is safe and known and step into the uncertain territory of our potential.

Each heroic journey is a gift, though it may come wrapped in struggle. If we embrace it, it will shape us, evolve us, and call forth a version of ourselves that is bolder, truer, and more impactful. We must answer the call to adventure, not only for our own growth but also on behalf of the world that awaits the gifts only we can bring.

FIND PURPOSE

Robert Byrne is credited with this profound insight: "The purpose of life is a life of purpose." This encapsulates what so many of us crave, especially as we enter midlife, seeking a life that transcends the mundane rhythms of "eat, work, sleep, repeat." Renowned purpose expert Richard Leider suggests that a universal purpose for all humans is "to give and to grow." Growth and contribution are not single acts; they are continuous cycles of becoming, where each step forward allows us to expand and offer more of ourselves. They lead to a deep sense of fulfillment and true happiness—and help ensure we don't have bitter regrets at the end of our lives.

Yet, our modern consumer society has conditioned us to do the opposite: to "grab and go" instead of "give and grow." We are urged to take as much as we can, accumulate wealth, and chase superficial goals. But this way of living—focused on consuming and hoarding—leaves a hollow legacy. Such a life may fill our bank accounts, but it leaves our souls empty, our impact negative or negligible. Living a life of purpose calls us to transcend self-centered accumulation and connect to what really matters in our lives.

There are different pathways to discovering purpose, each offering a unique lens. One way is intellectual—using frameworks like *Ikigai*, which guides us to align our strengths, passions, and the world's needs with work that sustains us. Another approach is spiritual, finding one's "calling" as a sacred duty or a path guided by something greater than oneself. Rick Warren's *The Purpose Driven Life*, one of the best-selling books of all time, resonates with millions because it roots purpose in faith and spirituality, a higher calling to serve. This is how Nilima discovered her purpose—by following the call of her spirit.

Then there is the path of experience, which is the way Raj found his purpose. Through the ups and downs of life, you learn what stirs your heart, lifts your spirit, and breaks you open. Philosopher Andrew Harvey speaks of the wisdom of "following our heartbreak," while Joseph Campbell advised us to "follow our bliss." Somewhere between these two powerful poles—between what pains us deeply and what brings us immense joy—lies our true purpose. It points us toward a life path that is both meaningful and fulfilling.

Raj shares:

> *I had a decent career, I was fulfilling my responsibilities, but I was also carrying a quiet, unacknowledged heartbreak. In the world of business and marketing, I saw practices that exploited people, degraded and objectified women, manipulated children into unhealthy habits—all in the name of profit. The more I witnessed, the more disturbed I felt. I realized I was living with a deep, unspoken sorrow, haunted by the gap between my work and my values. Despite my innate idealism, life had somehow conspired to place me in one of the most cynical of all professions: marketing.*

What do you see that others don't? What pains you in ways that leave others untouched? These are powerful questions on the path to purpose. For me, it was the harm I saw in my field. Marketing, which I'd once viewed as a respectable career, began to feel like an empty, even dishonorable pursuit. I often reflected on my father, who earned a PhD in agricultural science. I, on the other hand, had earned a PhD in marketing and was part of a profession that helped companies sell products that, in many cases, did more harm than good. My inner dialogue grew sharper and darker: My father had sought to end world hunger, while I peddled empty consumerism.

This heartbreak became my guide. I followed it, letting it show me where I felt ashamed, where I longed for a better way. For nearly twenty years, I expressed this shame by writing articles and books that exposed the darker sides of marketing. But I struggled to see a way forward until my mentor, Jag Sheth, posed a simple question. After reading a book proposal I had prepared titled The Shame of Marketing, *he remarked, "Raj, people need a solution, not just a diagnosis. What is the alternative?" His question was a pivot point, prompting me to look for what marketing could be, rather than merely exposing what it had become. I asked the question, "Is there a better way?" The answer to that question, regardless of context, is always yes.*

I retitled the book In Search of Marketing Excellence, *hoping to uncover companies that valued customers, respected their dignity, did not waste enormous amounts of money on ads, coupons, and junk mail, and contributed positively to society. My research uncovered businesses that thrived by placing human well-being at their core—companies beloved not just by their customers but by employees, suppliers, and communities. This exploration led me to identify the foundational pillars of what we would later call Conscious Capitalism: higher purpose, stakeholder integration, conscious leadership, and caring culture.*

In discovering these companies, I found the solution to my heartbreak. On the other side of our deepest pain lies our bliss. There was a particular moment when I was at a writing retreat in Pennsylvania, drafting a story about one of these businesses. Midway through, I felt tears welling up—tears of joy, an emotion I had never experienced in connection to my work. I turned to my coauthor David Wolfe and said, "I think my body is trying to tell me something—that this really matters.

I have never felt joy like this in my career. I think I just figured out what I want to do for the rest of my life: to fully understand and spread this way of being in business."

That moment, that tearful realization, was my body's wisdom breaking through years of numbness. I hadn't shed tears in decades, not since a deep emotional wound had led me to build a wall around my heart. For years, that wall had held me back from feeling. But here I was, vulnerable, alive, and, for the first time, connected to a purpose that felt true.

In that moment, I understood that business, done right, could be a vehicle for human dignity, compassion, and healing. I saw a way forward, a purpose that would guide the rest of my life. I now articulate that as, "My purpose is to elevate consciousness and open hearts for all of humanity, so that we can build a world where all life matters, and every life can thrive." Mine was no longer a career; it was a calling, a life mission.

Finding your purpose is not a single event; it is a journey, one that often involves heartbreak, struggle, and doubt. Yet on the other side of this journey is the bliss of living a life aligned with who you truly are, where your work is not just what you do, but an extension of your heart and soul. This is the legacy we can leave behind—a life in which we give, grow, and inspire others to do the same.

HEALING LEADERS PRACTICE
Discover Your Higher Purpose

The journey of self-expression begins with embracing your heroic journey (as discussed in Chapter 5) and continues here with discovering and living your higher purpose. This exercise is a brief exploration to help uncover the contours of this purpose. We'll use a worksheet to capture them (Figure 8).

Here's what to list in each quadrant:

QUADRANT 1: KNOWLEDGE AND SKILLS

Begin with your knowledge and skills—the abilities you have cultivated through education, training, and life experience. These may seem disconnected from your purpose, but often our journeys leave us better prepared than we think.

Nilima shares:

> *I trained in life sciences, biochemistry, and immunology, and when I later moved into communications, at first I thought this knowledge was of little use. But years later, when my husband was diagnosed with cancer, that scientific grounding became essential. I knew the immune system intimately, and with that knowledge, we developed a holistic and integrative medicine program for his recovery, based on psychoneuroimmunology, to keep his immune system in optimal condition. Later, I trained as a yoga teacher and coauthored* My Cancer Is Me: The Journey from Illness to Wholeness. *That became my work for the next decade—helping others on their journeys of healing.*

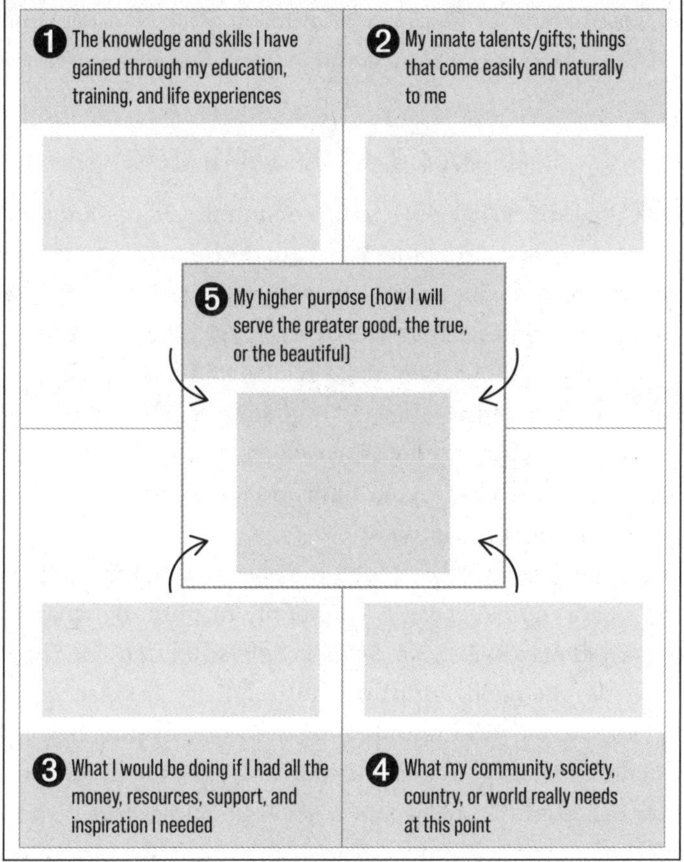

FIGURE 8. Discovering Your Higher Purpose

QUADRANT 2: INNATE GIFTS AND TALENTS

This quadrant is about your natural abilities—the gifts you were born with that come effortlessly. Nilima continues:

> *I am a dancer, a bodyworker. I could dance before I could walk. For years, it was just a hobby, but I eventually merged it with yoga and leadership work, creating Dancing the Five Elements to help others break free of limiting patterns. Movement became a way to embody authenticity and empowerment.*

QUADRANT 3: DREAMS WITH INFINITE RESOURCES

Now imagine that you have all the resources in the world. Money, time, and support are limitless. What would you do with this freedom? What would you create, contribute, or heal? Let your imagination wander. Follow your bliss, envisioning the impact you could make if you were unrestrained.

QUADRANT 4: WHAT THE WORLD NEEDS

Finally, ask yourself: What does your community, your industry, or the world desperately need right now? What are the injustices, the sorrows, the pain points that break your heart? What "social sadness" awaits your healing touch? What do you see that no one else sees? When you think, "Someone needs to do something about that," realize that someone is likely you.

Take your time filling out these four quadrants. The top two represent your natural gifts—your strengths, passions, and expertise. The bottom two reflect your heart's call—your bliss and heartbreak, the areas where you can create meaningful impact.

There's a good chance your life's purpose lies at the intersection of these four quadrants. Purpose is commonly inspired by what the Indic Knowledge System calls *Satyam*, *Shivam*, *Sundaram*, echoing the Platonic ideals: the true, the good, and the beautiful. Each of these represents a domain of human purpose: illuminating the truth, healing through goodness, or creating beauty. While your purpose may touch all three, often one shines brightest. Scholars and teachers may be drawn to the true, enriching the knowledge and wisdom of the world. Artists, on the other hand, are called to serve beauty, adding grace and inspiration to our lives.

Nilima reflects:

> ***I am clear that my purpose is rooted in the good. I bring the true and the beautiful to this work, but my core calling is to create a world of fairness, peace, and unity. My purpose is to end patriarchy and birth "synarchy"—a world where everyone plays their unique role in harmony.***

To synthesize these insights and help you discover your higher purpose, in the next exercise, we'll guide you in a dialogue with your higher self. Instead of letting your ego or analytical mind attempt to define your purpose, we encourage you to call upon this part of you—the part that already knows your true path. With this simple yet powerful practice, you can quiet your mind and connect directly with your higher self, finding deep answers to important life questions. In this case, you will use it to help articulate your purpose.

HEALING LEADERS PRACTICE
A Dialogue with Your Higher Self[2]

Allow yourself to let go of logic and self-doubt. Call upon your higher self with sincerity, and trust the words or images that come. Don't worry if it feels like imagination—after all, we don't truly know where any of our thoughts come from. If you approach this practice with an open heart, you'll receive insights of clarity and depth.

STEP 1: OPEN YOUR HEART AND EMBRACE YOUR INNER CHILD

To begin, create a sacred, quiet space for yourself. Keep a pen, paper, and your worksheet from the previous exercise nearby. Sit in an upright chair with both feet firmly on the ground, your back straight, and your eyes gently closed. Bring your awareness to your "here and now" self, settling into this moment.

Now, visualize your inner child—a younger version of yourself, who may have experienced fear, insecurity, or self-doubt. Picture this child standing before you, vulnerable yet deeply precious. Gently place your right hand on their left shoulder and your left arm around their waist,

holding them with love and reassurance. Offer this child self deep metta (loving-kindness, as we discussed in Chapter 3). Whisper to them: *May you be well. May you be happy. May you be free from all suffering.*

As you breathe, feel the integration of your adult self with this child self. Reconnect with their curiosity, joy, and sense of wonder. Let this playful, adventurous spirit infuse your heart. In this tender embrace, bring forth any question that is weighing on you about choices, dilemmas, or your "red thread" in life (the underlying theme, purpose, or passion that weaves through your experiences, connecting seemingly disparate events, interests, and relationships into a coherent narrative).

Ask yourself: *If I could ask an all-knowing being one question, what would it be?* Then articulate it with clarity. In this case, that question is: *What is my purpose?*

STEP 2: OPEN YOUR MIND AND ACCESS YOUR HIGHER SELF

Having brought your question into focus, slowly stand and move behind your chair. Visualize your ego self still sitting there, a reflection of your everyday mind. Now, take a step back and allow yourself to embody a new energy: that of your higher self. Stand with your feet shoulder-width apart and your back tall, feeling powerful, like an immovable mountain. Call upon your higher self, feeling its wisdom and clarity filling you.

Place your hands tenderly on the back of the chair, as though resting them on the shoulders of your ego self. Let your higher self channel the highest compassion and insight, like a gentle stream flowing from an endless source. Imagine you've opened a tap and wisdom is now flowing freely.

When you feel ready, sit down and begin to write. Let the words come without judgment or overthinking. Trust the clarity and intuition that is emerging through you. If you receive a word, a phrase, or a vision that resonates as your purpose, write it in the center of your worksheet.

STEP 3: INTEGRATING AND ACCEPTING YOUR POWER SYMBOL AND PERSONAL MYTH

When you've finished writing, close your eyes again and relax. Visualize yourself walking along a sunlit forest path. The air is fresh and fragrant, filled with birdsong, as a warm breeze stirs around you. You sense that something extraordinary awaits you on this path—something both powerful and sacred.

The trees thicken as you continue, but you walk with calm determination, feeling your will grow stronger. Soon, you step into a clearing where a mirror, draped with a veil, awaits. This mirror is the gateway to your truest self. In preparation, wash your hands and face in the nearby clear stream. Then, with reverence, lift the veil. Gaze into the mirror, and witness the vastness of your innermost self.

Approaching you through the mirror is a symbol—a being, object, or form that embodies your unique power. Look closely and see that this symbol represents you. The beauty, strength, and energy it radiates are your own. Allow this presence to merge with you, awakening every cell, filling you with the mantra: *I am this. I am this. I am this.*

This symbol is your touchstone, a reminder of who you are at your most powerful. Create a visual representation of it, whether a simple sketch or a full poster. Whenever you need grounding, return to this image: a reminder of the pleasure and potency of your essence. Let your right brain guide you in capturing the spirit of your power symbol—something that speaks to your heart, mind, and soul.

Now, having connected with your higher self and uncovered your purpose, reflect on what has emerged. Your logical self may wonder how this new purpose fits with the life you're already living. But this is where true transformation begins: by embracing a purpose that gently leads you from the comfort of the known into the uncharted territory of growth.

Take a moment to test the resonance of your purpose statement. Ask yourself:

- Does it ring true?
- Does it resonate at all three levels—my head, my heart, and my gut?
- Does it feel like it fits me? Does it also stretch me beyond where I stand today?
- Is this something I would be inspired to dedicate myself to for the next ten years?

Your answers should be a resounding *yes*. These questions are a way of "kicking the tires" on your higher-self dialogue, ensuring that what you have received is of profound and lasting value. If you have any lingering doubts, refine it until it feels like an authentic expression of who you are. When you feel alignment across your entire being, it's time to weave this purpose into the fabric of your life, integrating it with both your zone of excellence and your zone of genius.

This journey toward purpose often unfolds gradually. Once you make an inner commitment, the world around you responds in kind. The universe organizes itself in subtle, sometimes astonishing ways. You meet new people. Unexpected doors open. Looking back, Raj marvels at the people and opportunities that appeared in his life once he identified his purpose. Before long, the Conscious Capitalism movement was born—a vehicle to amplify that purpose beyond anything he could have imagined.

A commitment to purpose acts like a magnet, attracting relationships, ideas, and pathways that accelerate your journey. Once you infuse your life with purpose, even the most routine activities take on new meaning. Your zone of excellence—where you operate successfully but comfortably—can become a powerful foundation for something far more fulfilling. As you step further into your zone of genius, purpose gives you both courage and vision, enabling you to express yourself fully and make an indelible impact on the world.

CLAIM YOUR PERSONAL MYTH

This is the beginning of your personal myth—a conscious declaration of your leadership and your legacy. Take a moment to consider:

MY PURPOSE How will I live and express my purpose every day?

MY PRESENCE How will I embody and cultivate my truest self?

MY POWER How will I use my power in service of my purpose?

MY PLEASURE How will I find joy and fulfillment in this journey?

Tell your unique story in the third person. Who is this person? What unique gift do they possess? Where are they heading, and what purpose fuels them? What challenges stand in their way, and what strengths will they draw upon to overcome them?

Our higher purpose is not an external goal to reach but an inner truth to express, to live, to become. Allow these words to be a guide, a reminder that the power to express yourself fully lies within, waiting for you to step forward and claim it. Go forth with courage. This is the process of expressing yourself, of living fully, and of transforming the world through your higher purpose.

CONSCIOUS LEADERS SPEAK
Express Yourself

To express yourself is not merely to speak or perform. It is to allow what is true and alive within you to move into the world. Expression is the bridge between your soul and your service. And yet, for many of us, it's blocked—not by inability, but by fear: fear of judgment, rejection, failure, or ridicule. The conscious leaders we spoke with show us that true expression is not about ego; it's about alignment. It's about clearing the channel so your gifts can flow freely and help others come alive.

For Simon Cohen, expression is quite literally a healing force. When energy gets stuck in the body, it causes pain. When it flows, healing happens. "Expression is about letting energy move. When you don't express what's inside—joy, sadness, fear—it gets trapped in the body. That stuck energy becomes a blockage. I call it emotional constipation. That energy has to go somewhere. If you don't let it out, it can turn into illness. But when you release it, it becomes healing. That's why I sing, dance, cry, laugh, shout—not for performance, but for health. Expression clears the channel. Even now, just talking to you, my back pain is gone. That's the power of expression. It moves energy. And when energy moves, healing begins."

Doug Rauch reminds us that love, unexpressed, is inert. "It's not enough to feel love—we have to express it. I think of my grandsons. I can love them silently, but if I don't say it, show it, act on it, what do they actually receive? Life doesn't just call us to feel; it calls us to show up, to act. Expression is how we come alive—and it's how we help others come alive

too. There's a lot that happens between our ears. We think, we feel, we imagine—but at some point, it has to leave our minds and enter the world. Expression is not just communication—it's transformation." Doug points out that growth always carries risk. But so does staying safe. "I've found that the pain of missed opportunity—of not stepping into something because of fear—is far greater than the pain of failure."

Kristin Engvig found healing in visibility—in choosing to let herself be seen, joyful and whole. "There was a time I didn't want to be seen. I didn't want to do interviews. I wanted to disappear. But part of healing is showing up—letting people see your joy, your tears. When I dance, I feel free. One day, I posted a video of myself dancing with sticks in India. My mother called and said, 'Kristin, you looked so happy!' I cried. For years, I thought my joy was too much for her. But in that moment, I realized: She loves me exactly as I am. That healed something deep in me."

Marisa Lazo's journey to self-expression came when she stopped performing and aligned with her deeper purpose. "You can't express yourself fully if you're not being authentic. Otherwise, you're just performing someone else's expectations—what your family, your culture, or your society told you to be. Finding my purpose gave me clarity. I stopped pretending. I stopped trying to meet everyone's expectations. I could finally say no to what didn't matter—because I had something bigger to say yes to." Marisa has stayed true to herself even in the high-profile role of being a judge on *Shark Tank Mexico*. "I told them, 'I'm a dolphin, not a shark.' They said, 'That's exactly why we want you.' And now I cry on national television, and I don't care. I want people to see that you can build a successful business with kindness, tears, and joy."

Morad Fareed's powerful reflections remind us that expression follows authenticity—and sometimes, it floods in after years of internal war. "The war was this: Why am I not enough? Why do I spend all my energy trying to prove myself? Now I know—I am enough. I don't need to impress or outperform. I just need to be real. Once the pain is transmuted, expression becomes effortless. It rains. It pours. It's beyond your control; it just needs to come out. And when it does, you realize: The war is over. I know now that I have a unique voice. My experience—everything I've been through—is not just for me. It's for others too. I'm no longer trying to fit in. I'm just showing up."

Gervase Warner's voice echoes the longing many leaders feel when their deepest gifts remain partly unexpressed. "Right now, I don't feel like I'm fully sharing my gifts with the world. I'm advising, mentoring, contributing—but I'm not leading. There's a part of me that wants to create again, to make something happen. I'm still discovering what that next expression looks like. But I know this: It will be authentic. It will be led from the heart."

Avivah Wittenberg-Cox sees her writing as both self-therapy and public service—an alchemical act of expression and meaning-making. "Writing is self-therapy. It's meditation. It's how I meet myself and understand what's going on—in the world and in my own life. It's how I find the nugget of meaning that might be useful to others. The more personal I get, the more universally it resonates. That's the magic of real expression—it becomes a mirror for others."

For Timothy Henry, expression has always been a search for purpose across disciplines and cultures. "I didn't really have a comfort zone. I was always moving—California, Oxford, New York, Tokyo. I was searching for something. That search became an expression of who I am. Even in my thirties, I was asking: What is my calling? What is the voice of the Spirit inside me? That's what led me to Joseph Campbell, Parker Palmer, and eventually to purpose. It's what led me to Conscious Capitalism."

John Mackey views expression as the act of answering life's deeper call. "Everyone is called to a hero's journey. Your soul is calling you to wake up, to evolve. If you don't answer that call, you end up living a life that feels unfulfilling. The problem is, we're afraid—of failure, disapproval, even success. So we play it safe. But growth seldom comes from playing life safely. Expression is how we respond to the soul's summons. And it's never over. Our interior universe is infinite—just like the cosmos."

For Kip Tindell, expression has always been about enthusiasm and congruence—doing what you love, and letting that speak for itself. "There are things I do well, and things I don't—but I've been lucky to build a business that reflected my passions and values. And I think that made it easier for everyone around me to thrive. I love organizing closets. I love people. I love building something meaningful. If you're comfortable with yourself and you're not driven by insecurity, it's easy to express yourself with enthusiasm and humility."

Together, these voices form a living symphony of what it means to express yourself—not from ego or ambition, but from essence. To express yourself is to give the world a gift that only you can offer. It is to say, with humility and conviction: *This is who I am. This is what I came to give.*

Expressing your purpose is a vital step in reclaiming your true self—but purpose cannot carry its full power if it arises from a fragmented being. To live a purpose-driven life, you must become whole.

In the next step, you will turn inward to integrate the parts of yourself that have been hidden, cut off, or denied—your inner masculine and feminine, the wise elder and the vulnerable child. This is the work of healing the inner divides, of becoming *complete*, so that your purpose flows not just from your voice but from the full depth and unity of your being.

CHAPTER 7

Complete Your Self

The divine feminine and the sacred masculine are not outside of us; they are the eternal polarities seeking reunion within our own soul.

—ANDREW HARVEY

The next step in this transformative journey is to *complete* yourself. Becoming whole is about embracing and integrating all aspects of who you are—balancing your inner energies, harmonizing polarities, and reclaiming your full self.

One of the greatest gifts we can give ourselves and others is wholeness. To be well, to flourish, to complete the heroic journey again and again, we must pass through the gateway of wholeness. There is no shortcut; only by integrating all parts of ourselves can we experience true well-being.

Everything that exists has its counterpart. Recall the identity exercise from Chapter 2, where you chose one descriptor and released its opposite. While that initial step was essential, true wholeness asks us to move beyond singular choices, embracing the essence of the opposite quality as well. This integration is the key to wholeness. When we overidentify with one part of ourselves and reject its counterpart, we push it into the shadows, judging it as wrong or inferior. Eventually, what's been denied manifests as a distortion or imbalance, revealing itself through conflict, emotional turmoil, or even physical illness. To heal, we must bring these rejected parts back into the light, integrate their core qualities, and, in doing so, complete ourselves.

Take, for example, masculine and feminine energies. If you identify as a woman, wholeness doesn't mean rejecting the masculine. Instead, it requires finding and embracing the essence of masculine energy and weaving it into your womanhood. Only by doing so can you be complete as a woman—and the same is true in reverse. Becoming whole is not about shedding parts of yourself; it's about expanding yourself.

This path is one we must each take individually. Partners—whether in marriage or other close relationships—must first come into their own wholeness before then can bring that fullness to each other. Imagine the freedom of a relationship in which neither partner is looking to the other to "complete" them. To walk as a whole person alongside another whole person is one of life's most fulfilling, joyful experiences. Without wholeness, relationships degenerate into codependency and cycles of unmet need and pain.

People sometimes admire relationships where two souls seem to have merged into one. But if "one plus one equals one," someone's essence has been lost in the union. Ideally, one plus one should be far greater than two. When two whole people come together, their potential magnifies, and the possibilities for creation, joy, and growth become boundless.

THE FOUR-FOLD SELF

Achieving psychological wholeness requires embracing the *four-fold self*, composed of two polarities that anchor and harmonize our inner world (Figure 9). The central idea is that each of us contains four core energies: the masculine (yang or animus), the feminine (yin or anima), the elder/parent, and the child. Wholeness depends on maintaining balance among them—not only within individuals,

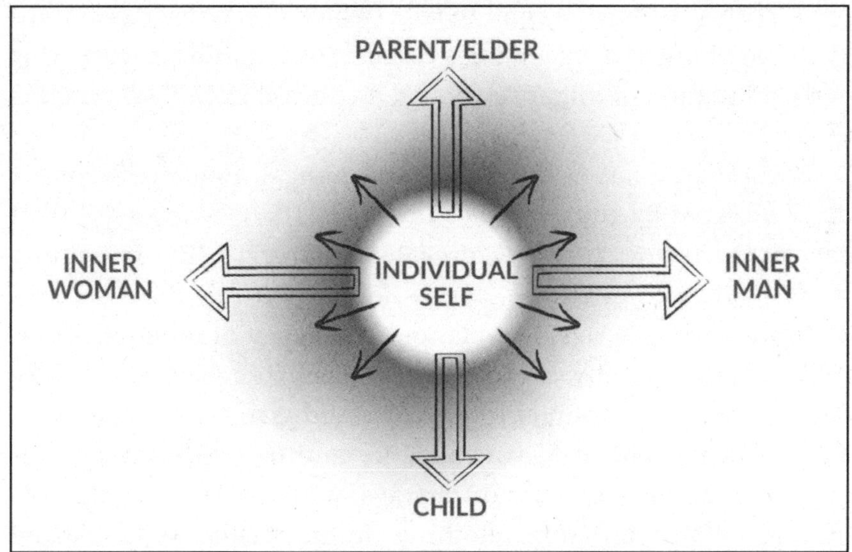

FIGURE 9. Psychological Wholeness—The Four-Fold Self

but across families, organizations, communities, nations, and the planet itself. When any of these energies becomes over- or under-expressed, the imbalance must be identified and the expression of that energy recalibrated to restore harmony.

Many traditions highlight this balance, including the yin and yang in Chinese philosophy, the anima and animus in Western psychology, and the concept of *Ardhanarishvara* in Indic thought. Variations of "four-fold theory" or the "four-fold way" also appear in many approaches to integration or healing. For example, Eric Berne's Transactional Analysis encourages us to become aware adults by integrating the elder (or "parent") and child energies within us, while Carl Jung taught that becoming whole involves the process of individuation—not only integrating the ego and the shadow but also embracing, for men, the inner feminine (the anima), and for women, the inner masculine (the animus), as part of the journey toward psychological completeness.

Consider the United States, a nation founded predominantly on masculine energy. The Founding Fathers chose to exclude women from governance and economic life, granting them neither property rights nor the right to vote (which was not secured until 1920). Without the balancing presence of feminine energy, this early masculine dominance shaped a cultural DNA that remains today.

Each energy has both healthy and unhealthy expressions, as demonstrated by the examples in Figure 10. In many aspects of American culture, we see a prevalence of unhealthy masculine traits—hyper-competition, aggression, and a relentless pursuit of dominance—alongside a marked deficiency of feminine qualities such as empathy, compassion, and collaboration. Unhealthy elder energy also abounds, often expressed as rigidity, dogmatism, and authoritarianism. Meanwhile, the country's child energy frequently manifests in immature ways, with adults struggling to mature emotionally and retaining the impulsive, self-centered traits of youth. These are all signs of a lack of balance and wholeness, reflected in an increasingly fractured society.

The key to psychological wholeness is learning to cultivate the healthy aspects of each of these energies, while recognizing and avoiding or transforming their shadow sides. By mastering these four aspects of the self, you can begin to live as a complete, integrated individual.

	MASCULINE ENERGY	FEMININE ENERGY	ELDER ENERGY	CHILD ENERGY	
HEALTHY	STRENGTH & FOCUS	COMPASSION & INCLUSION	PURPOSE & WISDOM	INNOCENCE & JOY	★
UNHEALTHY	VIOLENT & SELFISH	NEEDY & SMOTHERING	DOGMA & DIVISION	INFANTILE & SELF-INDULGENT	

FIGURE 10. The Energy Matrix

THE RISE OF THE FEMININE

Many of today's polycrises can be traced, at least in part, to an excess of unchecked masculine energy. Left unbalanced, healthy masculine qualities (such as strength, structure, decisiveness, and resilience) can devolve into aggression, domination, and the drive to win at all costs—turning everything into a battle. In the United States, for instance, nearly every significant problem prompts a declaration of war:

- War on Poverty
- War on Drugs
- War on Crime
- War on Terror
- War on Cancer
- War on Inflation
- War on Government Waste
- War on Homelessness
- War on Obesity
- War on Human Trafficking
- War on Hunger

None of these wars have succeeded. The War on Drugs alone is estimated to have cost the country $1–1.5 trillion between 1971 and 2020, with millions incarcerated but little evidence of its underlying goals being achieved. In fact, the number of drug overdose deaths each year surged from about 6,000 in 1970 to over 100,000 in 2021, with drug availability and use also increasing.

Declaring war on a problem is a classically masculine response—one we are finally beginning to move beyond. Europe provides a striking contrast. From 1346 to 1946, European countries fought over 1,200 wars with one another. Since 1946, however, no wars have erupted between Western European nations. Europe, in many ways, has integrated feminine energy into its politics more effectively than the United States, a country that has been engaged in conflict for over 90 percent of its history. In Northern European social democracies, women enjoy equal rights and family support is robust. In 2003, Robert Kagan captured this difference by saying, "On major strategic and international questions today, Americans are from Mars, and Europeans are from Venus."[1]

There is growing recognition that feminine energy has been missing not only from politics, but from business and leadership more broadly. Books, research, and studies have highlighted how qualities that come more naturally to women are precisely those most needed in leadership today. A McKinsey study led by Joanna Barsh interviewed hundreds of successful leaders and found that the most effective qualities identified were often those considered more innate to women. Based on these insights, the researchers developed a model called *Centered Leadership*, reflecting how many women naturally lead.[2]

In *The Athena Doctrine: How Women (and the Men Who Think like Them) Will Rule the Future*, John Gerzema and Michael D'Antonio share the results of a large-scale global survey, in which two-thirds of respondents said they believed the world would be a better place if men thought more like women. When the authors examined perceptions of leadership effectiveness, they found a clear trend: Qualities traditionally considered "feminine"—such as empathy, collaboration, intuition, patience, and flexibility—were widely recognized as vital to success in leadership, business, and society. By contrast, traditionally "masculine" traits—such as aggression, analytical thinking, independence, and pride—were negatively correlated with effective leadership. Happiness, ethics, and morality aligned even more strongly with feminine traits.

This data reveals the pressing need to elevate feminine qualities in leadership. Of course, achieving this doesn't mean replacing all the men with women. While it's crucial to bring more women into boardrooms and executive roles, it's equally important for men to cultivate and express their own feminine traits. Men and women must rise together, with men embracing their full emotional and relational capacities, and women stepping into leadership roles in ways that honor their natural strengths.

In the past, women have often felt pressured to adopt masculine behaviors to succeed. Leaders like Indira Gandhi, Margaret Thatcher, and Golda Meir exemplified this: Gandhi was often described as "the only man in her cabinet," Thatcher as Britain's "Iron Lady," and Meir as Israel's "Iron Lady." These women, operating in male-dominated environments, adopted hyper-masculine traits to survive and dominate.

The world today calls for a different approach—one in which men, women, and nonbinary people can lead with balance and wisdom, combining the strengths of both masculine and feminine energy to create a more compassionate, collaborative, and humane world.

INTEGRATE YOUR POLARITIES

Barry Johnson's framework of polarity thinking is an invaluable tool for resolving seemingly intractable dilemmas.[3] It's no exaggeration to say that embracing this perspective can transform your life, your relationships, and your leadership.

Dilemmas often arise when we are asked to choose between two positive options. Polarity thinking reveals that many aspects of life exist as interdependent pairs rather than isolated choices. Take breathing: Both inhaling and exhaling are essential to the rhythm of life. Asking someone to choose between inhaling and exhaling would be absurd—without both in concert, life would cease.

So why do we think we can choose between the masculine and the feminine? These energies are also interdependent, sustaining and balancing one another. The attempt to separate them—prioritizing one while discarding the other—has left us, as a species and as a planet, gasping for balance and harmony.

Consider another common polarity: justice and mercy. A system focused solely on justice would be unforgiving, rigid, and harshly punitive. This could have tragic consequences, with people facing extreme punishments for minor offenses with extenuating circumstances. On the other hand, a system that prioritized only mercy would risk allowing harmful behaviors to proliferate unchecked, fostering a culture where crime escalates. Justice and mercy must temper each other; without both, we inevitably encounter the destructive side of each.

Polarity thinking invites us to embrace a dynamic balance, honoring both sides of any duality as essential to wholeness. By learning to integrate them, we find a path to resilience, compassion, and a fuller, more expansive life.

Integrate Your Masculine–Feminine

Each of us was born of both a mother and a father, inheriting qualities and energies from each. Gender serves a biological purpose in reproduction, but it should not limit us or hinder our capacity for wholeness.

Major wisdom traditions acknowledge the duality and complementarity of these energies. In the yin-yang symbol from Chinese philosophy, yin contains a spark of yang, and yang holds a trace of yin—they are not separate, but interwoven. When our limited human consciousness polarizes, embracing one energy and rejecting the other, imbalance and distortion take hold. In traditional Chinese medicine, the first step in healing is to assess the imbalance between yin and yang, before treating the body with herbs, acupuncture, or qigong to restore harmony. This concept applies across all systems: individuals, families, organizations, even nations. The essential question is: Which energy is overexpressed, and which is underexpressed? Our task is to restore dynamic equilibrium.

The Indic tradition offers a parallel archetype in Ardhanarishvara, the half-male, half-female deity representing Shiva (consciousness) and Shakti (creative power). This iconic form reveals that we are, by nature, both masculine and feminine, as inseparable as heat and light in fire.

Polarity mapping offers a powerful way to integrate the masculine and feminine within us, enabling us to harness the strengths of each. To begin, create a four-quadrant matrix with masculine and feminine energies on either side. The top two quadrants represent the healthy expressions of each energy, while the lower two reflect their shadow or unhealthy forms (Figure 11). The goal is to stay above the line, in the positive quadrants, and avoid falling below, where strengths turn into weaknesses or destructive traits.

To step into your full power, you must become a whole person by integrating both your masculine and feminine sides. Healthy masculine qualities include clarity, assertiveness, focus, direction,

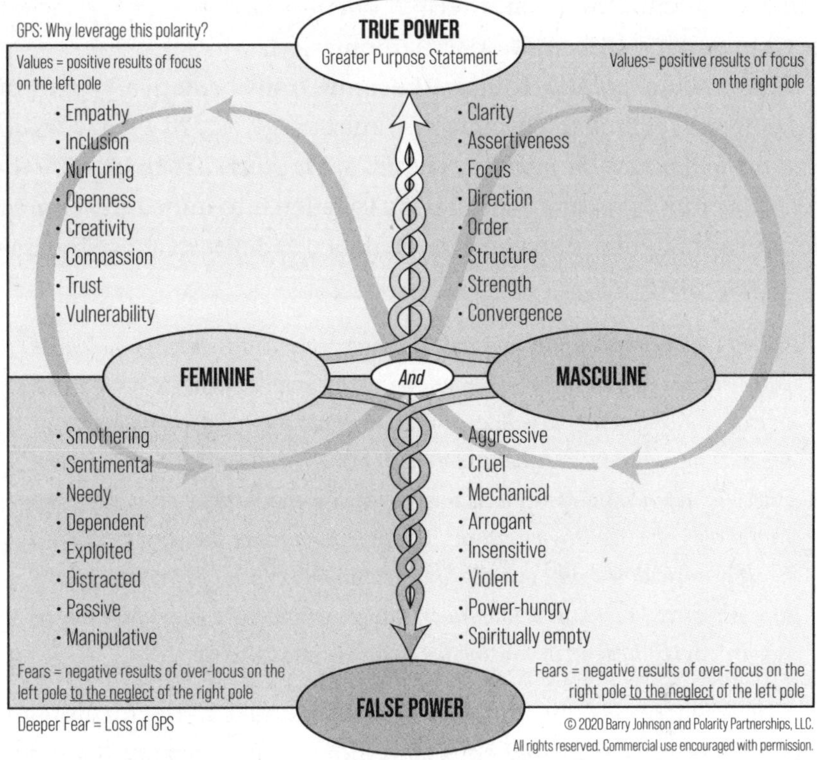

FIGURE 11. The Masculine–Feminine Polarity Map. Adapted with permission from Barry Johnson.

order, structure, strength, and convergence. But when we rely excessively on these traits and neglect the feminine, they can distort into aggression, cruelty, rigidity, arrogance, insensitivity, and an unyielding drive for power.

Healthy feminine qualities—empathy, inclusion, nurturing, openness, creativity, compassion, trust, and vulnerability—are equally essential. Nilima recalls teaching a group of female leaders at a multinational bank about these qualities. They were stunned, saying, "These qualities were drained out of us long ago. We don't even know how to find them anymore." Many of today's workplaces do not reward, measure, or value these traits, creating environments that stifle the feminine. Conversely, as with hyper-masculinity, an overemphasis on feminine energy can take us below the line into hyper-femininity: smothering, neediness, dependency, lack of focus, passivity, and emotional manipulation.

Here's where polarity thinking becomes transformative. When you feel yourself leaning too heavily into one energy, ask: *In what ways am I failing to manifest the healthy qualities of the other?* Try to identify the early warning signs that indicate you've fallen into unhealthy expressions of either energy, so you can rebalance and return above the line.

Nilima shares:

> *When I fall below the line, I become needy, experiencing what psychologists call "learned helplessness"—something many women struggle with. I find myself wanting others to validate me or do things for me. Recognizing neediness as my warning sign helps me catch myself before going further down. Barry Johnson suggests that at this point, you should take an action step in the opposite, healthy quadrant. For me, the answer lies in self-care—a healthy masculine trait I already have within me. When I feel needy, I practice self-care: I schedule a massage, connect with people who uplift me, or reward myself instead of waiting for someone else to do so.*

These warning signs and action steps can take many forms. Each person may have multiple cues that indicate they're slipping below the line, just as they may have various ways to rebalance. This process resembles a Möbius strip, cycling between poles in a fluid loop through all four quadrants. In the beginning, we may fall very low, experiencing the worst of both worlds. With practice, we learn to recognize our warning signs and return more quickly to the healthy quadrants. Over time, the entire loop shifts upward, allowing us to spend longer periods in the "sweet spot" of balance.

Nilima continues:

> *If I overfocus on masculine qualities, I risk falling into hyper-masculinity. Growing up as "my father's daughter," I was very focused on getting good grades and succeeding professionally in a masculinized world. When I remain in this mode for too long, I begin to lose touch with empathy, compassion, and vulnerability.*
>
> *My early warning sign is judgment. I start feeling superior, noticing flaws in everyone else. When I catch myself in judgment, I know I've gone too far into the masculine. To restore balance, I take an action*

step toward the healthy feminine, which for me is compassion—a trait I've practiced for years. Compassion is the perfect antidote to judgment, offering me a completely different way to see others. By moving between self-care and compassion, I stay in my "presence," grounded in a balance of self-care and empathy. When I lose this balance, I fall below the line into a painful mix of judgment and neediness—the worst place to be, a true "dance of death."

Raj reflects on his own upbringing:

When I was growing up, in my family we had the worst of both worlds. The men were aggressive, cruel, and arrogant, while the women were needy, dependent, and disempowered. Neither side had integrated the healthy qualities of the other, leaving us trapped in a cycle of dysfunction.

This journey of integration is essential for reclaiming balance, resilience, and wholeness in our lives. Polarity mapping is a tool that helps us recognize our early warning signs and make deliberate choices to restore harmony, cultivating a life where masculine and feminine, strength and compassion, coexist in dynamic interchange. In this way, we discover our true power—integrated, balanced, and whole.

HEALING LEADERS PRACTICE
Identify Your Warning Signs and Action Steps

Identify the early warning sign that indicates you are becoming hyper-feminine. Then, determine the action step you will commit to to return to healthy masculine. Similarly, identify the early warning sign that indicates you are becoming hyper-masculine, and choose the action step you will commit to to return to healthy feminine.

A word about action steps: Try to identify a strong point or trait—something you are already good at. This will make it easier for you to snap out of the negative emotion or behavior that is pulling you down. Use that to return yourself "above the line." Once back in a healthy place, you can leverage other strengths from the top two quadrants to get yourself back in the saddle of presence and flow.

Integrate Your Elder–Child

Now, let's explore the elder–child dynamic. The goal here is to find the right balance between your elder (or parent) and child energies, so you can access the best of both and live in your true strength. When these energies are unbalanced, they pull us into false, manipulative power. Figure 12 shows the polarity map for these two energies.

Let's begin with the positive qualities of the elder: meaning and purpose, legacy and impact, forgiveness, acceptance, transcendence, unity, expansiveness, and selflessness. These are the gifts that the wise elder brings to a community, and they are also the gifts that your inner wise self can bring to you. However, if you neglect

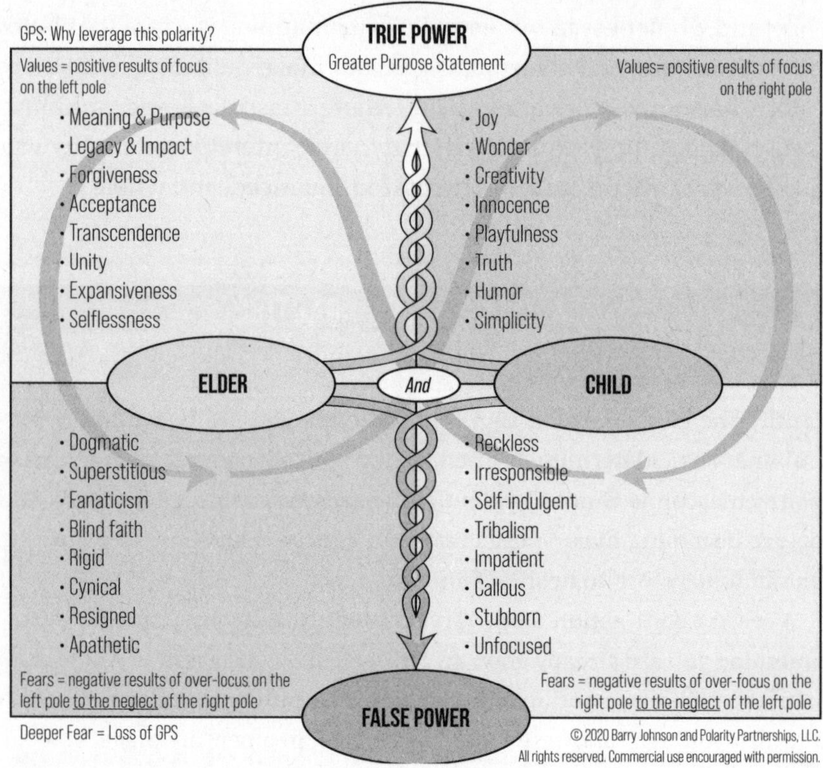

FIGURE 12. The Elder–Child Polarity Map. Adapted with permission from Barry Johnson.

your childlike qualities, focusing solely on elder energy, you risk falling below the line into its negative expressions: rigidity, dogmatism, fanaticism, cynicism, resignation, apathy.

Now consider the positive qualities of the child: joy, wonder, creativity, innocence, playfulness, truth, humor, and simplicity. These qualities bring lightness and spontaneity—but if you focus solely on childlike joy and neglect responsibility, you may fall below the line into immaturity, where recklessness, impatience, self-indulgence, and distraction take over.

The key to integrating elder and child energies lies in learning to "inhale and exhale" between them, finding a balance between wisdom and playfulness and staying above the line. Rely too heavily on one, and you're likely to slip into imbalance.

Start by reflecting on your childlike qualities. Do you notice any tendencies that may pull you below the line, such as distraction, restlessness, or impatience? If you find yourself feeling scattered or unfocused, it's a clue to reconnect with your elder energy, finding a sense of purpose and clarity by concentrating on what truly matters.

Conversely, if you lean too far into elder energy, you risk becoming rigid, seeing only your perspective and dismissing others. If someone challenges your beliefs, rather than shutting down, invoke your inner child's openness and curiosity and engage them in honest dialogue.

Balance emerges when you can exhale into curiosity about others and inhale back into your own purpose. How can you tell when you've slipped below the line? You'll feel both dogmatic and unfocused—a sign that presence has been lost and integration is needed.

Raj says:

> *One of my early warning signs of falling into immature child energy is impatience. I aspire to be more patient, so when I notice impatience arising, I look to healthy elder qualities and choose acceptance. Acceptance is a powerful antidote, helping us collaborate and move at a more natural pace, rather than forcing others to meet our timelines or expectations.*

The next time you notice yourself becoming rigid or controlling, try applying playfulness as a remedy. Invite feedback from those around you—your partner, family members, or colleagues. They can help you recognize habitual "below the line" behaviors and see how these patterns may be affecting you and others.

Integrating elder and child energy in this way offers a path to balance, creativity, and true inner presence. By staying attuned to your early warning signs and responding with conscious, healthy action, you can fully embody both the wisdom of the elder and the joy of the child, living in harmony and wholeness.

Become the Wise Fool of Tough Love

When we integrate our masculine and feminine energies, as well as our elder and child aspects, we become a "Wise Fool of Tough Love." This phrase came to Nilima as she sought to distill the essence of *Shakti Leadership*. She asked herself, "What is this journey really about?" In the Indic tradition, a great scripture, or *Upanishad*, ends with a *maha-vaakya*—a grand pronouncement that encapsulates its teaching in a single line. For *Shakti Leadership*, this line is "becoming the Wise Fool of Tough Love." This is what it means to become psychologically whole:

- The *Wise* is the elder self, embodying wisdom, purpose, and clarity.
- The *Fool* is the curious, joyful, playful child within us, unafraid to make mistakes and learn.
- *Tough* is the inner masculine warrior, setting boundaries, saying "no," and fighting for what matters.
- *Love* is the inner feminine, the nurturing force that holds space, collaborates, and cares.

The concept of the Wise Fool of Tough Love serves as a powerful lens for addressing life's challenges. If you're stuck in a situation, chances are it's because you're not being wise enough, foolish enough, tough enough, or loving enough. By identifying what's missing and restoring that balance, you unlock solutions.

Reflecting on their own lives, Nilima shares that her journey has been about integrating "tough" and "love," while Raj says his path has centered around integrating "fool" and "tough." Nilima found her own masculine-feminine balance through her marriage, while Raj's life was strongly shaped by his very different relationships with each of his parents.

Raj explains:

> *Wisdom and love came naturally to me, but toughness and foolishness took conscious effort. I've had to actively cultivate my healthy masculine side for toughness and remember to stay connected with my inner child. I have a good sense of humor but often lack playfulness. This balance is unique to each person.*

Becoming a Wise Fool of Tough Love is the culmination of the journey toward a balanced, whole self. This archetype invites us as leaders, partners, and individuals to embody wisdom, child-like wonder, courage, and compassion—all essential to living with integrity and authenticity.

CONSCIOUS LEADERS SPEAK
Complete Yourself

Completion is not about arriving at perfection. It is not about having all the answers, or finally "fixing" ourselves. It is about wholeness—integrating what we've separated, accepting what we've disowned, embracing the fullness of who we are. For conscious leaders, this often involves reconciling the masculine and feminine, the adult and inner child, the intellect and the soul. Completion is not static; it's an ongoing dance between parts that are learning to live together in harmony. What follows are reflections from leaders who are walking—and embodying—that journey.

Doug Rauch reframes "completion" as integration—bringing the hidden and rejected parts of ourselves into the light. "I'd rephrase this step—not 'complete yourself' as if something's missing, but 'embrace all parts of yourself.' The Jungian idea rings true for me: Everything is already in us—the light and the dark, the masculine and the feminine. The journey isn't about adding anything new. It's about accepting what's already

there. We all have parts we'd rather not see—the awkward, the petty, the fearful. But they don't go away just because we ignore them. They go underground—and that's when they start running the show. When we bring them into the light, we stop hiding. We become more trustworthy, more real."

Avivah Wittenberg-Cox speaks of completion or integration as a sacred harvest. "I'm in what I call Q3—between fifty and seventy-five. A stage of harvest. I've done the building, the raising, the proving. Now it's about integrating, about becoming whole. That means letting go of old structures, embracing softness, and inviting joy. I've spent decades helping companies balance masculine and feminine leadership. Now I'm working on that within myself—honoring both the Wise and the Fool, the elder and the child. That's where wholeness lives."

John Mackey shares how his journey has been one of softening the warrior and expanding the heart. "I've always had that masculine drive—competitive, ambitious, strong. What I had to learn was how to open my heart. Through A Course in Miracles, MDMA, and deep inner work, I've been integrating that other side—love, empathy, presence. That's real power: when love and strength come together. It's also the foundation of conscious leadership. In every decision, I try to practice Win-Win-Win: a win for me, a win for you, and a win for the greater whole. That's masculine clarity guided by feminine compassion."

Timothy Henry grew up with the message that toughness equals strength. Completion meant rewiring that belief. "I was raised with a hyper-masculine energy: tough it out, suffer through, be the warrior. I was proud of how much pain I could take. But over time, I saw how limiting that was. I consciously worked on cultivating my nurturing side—what we now call feminine intelligence. Being a father was a big part of that. I became the emotional caregiver in my kids' lives, which helped complete something in me. At some point I said, 'I don't just want to be a warrior—I want to be a spiritual warrior.' That shift opened my heart and made me more whole."

Kristin Engvig found wholeness through sacred structure—routines that support her feminine flow. "I realized I needed the masculine structure to support my feminine flow. That was the missing piece. Now, I create containers—disciplined routines—so I can rest, be creative, and lead from love. It's about inner balance. Every night, I do a healing meditation for the little Kristin. I don't forget her. I hold space for the parent and the child inside me. That's how I feel complete."

For Marisa Lazo, completion means honoring her masculine strength and feminine softness—as well as the ancestral threads that shaped her. "I had developed a strong masculine side—maybe from being close to my father, or surviving in a man's world. But integrating my feminine—my softness, my intuition, my vulnerability—was essential to feel whole. Men struggle more with this. They're not encouraged to embrace their feminine. In our foundation, we help shift that—so men feel proud of their tenderness, the way we women had to reclaim ours."

For Ed Freeman, completion involved shedding cultural blinders and integrating the emotional and relational self. "I grew up in a sexist, racist culture in the South. It took time—and the help of close relationships—for me to see that clearly and begin to change. I often say—half-jokingly—that I'm a woman trapped in a man's body, because most of my close friends are women. But it's not about gender—it's about integration. About living a whole, authentic life."

Kip Tindell reflects on how his mother's love shaped his wholeness—and how he brought that ethos into his company. "My mother was probably my best friend. We'd talk until three or four in the morning about life and business. I trusted her more than anyone. I'm a big feminist. At one point, seventeen of our top twenty-one leaders were women—not by design, just by merit. I honestly think women are better at most things than men, except maybe upper body strength. And we used that to dominate the world. Go figure."

For Gervase Warner, wholeness means showing up with both strategy and softness, logic and love. "My wife Les brings the tough love, the heart, the insight. And I've come to see that all of me belongs: the playful side, the strategic side, the loving side. Wholeness isn't about suppressing parts of yourself. It's about letting them all emerge with integrity."

Morad Fareed's completion came when he let go of control and embraced the natural improvisation of life. "I used to lead everything from the mind—solve, intervene, control. Now I let it breathe. I don't need to dominate. I'm playing jazz with others—everyone leads when it's their turn. I don't care about being right. I care about keeping things playful and

kind. That's what my soul wants: to have fun, to lift the energy in a room. It's not performance—it's presence."

Simon Cohen reminds us that completion is not always solitary. It's also found in love, connection, and shared presence. "Completion can come from within—but for me, it's often awakened in connection. I feel most whole when I'm brainstorming with my team, or holding my wife's hand by the ocean. It's not just an inner state. It's relational. Completion is peace. It's when you look in the mirror and smile. It's not about perfection. It's about presence."

These leaders show us that completing yourself is not about becoming someone else. It is about becoming fully, joyfully, honestly yourself. It is about gathering the pieces of your life, your lineage, your longing—and letting them belong to one whole story. Not a perfect story. But a true one.

Next, we move to the culminating step of this journey: *healing* yourself. All the steps you have taken so far are part of your healing; skipping over any of them creates its own kind of wound to your being. In the next chapter, we will discuss three important aspects to complete the healing journey: healing your story, your body, and your psychic wounds and traumas.

CHAPTER 8

Heal Yourself

Your wound is probably not your fault,
but your healing is your responsibility.
—DENICE FROHMAN

This entire journey is ultimately about *healing* yourself. Every step we've taken together is essential to the healing process.

Is healing needed in the world? Absolutely. We believe that healing is the meta need of our times. Humanity has made remarkable progress over the past 200 years—higher incomes, longer lives, increased literacy—but suffering persists. The World Bank estimates that one in ten people globally live in extreme poverty, surviving on less than $3.00 a day. Nearly half the world's population lives on less than $8.30 a day.[1] And of course, financial security doesn't guarantee happiness. Many people in developed countries—especially in the West—grapple with deep psychological distress. We are living in an era marked by epidemic levels of anxiety and depression. In the United States, a survey found that over a quarter of young adults (aged eighteen to twenty-four) had seriously contemplated suicide during the COVID-19 pandemic.[2]

Beyond human hardship, there is immense suffering in the animal world—particularly in factory farming systems—and in nature itself. The sixth mass extinction in Earth's history, and the first caused by human activity, is currently in progress. Species are disappearing at rates estimated to be 100 to 1,000 times higher than natural background rates.[3] Our communities are fractured. Our planet's natural systems are under great stress.

With all the suffering in the world, we are each called to become forces for healing. But we cannot offer what we haven't yet cultivated within. To help others heal, we must first heal ourselves. That's the purpose of the journey you are taking, culminating in this final step: exploring what needs to be healed in each of us.

If you scan your body, you may find physical scars—marks from childhood injuries, perhaps. Yet most of our scars are invisible: emotional, psychological, hidden from view. And rarely do we pause to tend to them. This chapter invites you to do exactly that—to acknowledge those scars and give them the care they require to heal.

There are three core dimensions to this process:

HEAL YOUR STORY

The quality of our lives is often shaped by the stories we tell ourselves. Life can feel chaotic—even meaningless at times—but we have the power to reshape it by telling a meaningful story about our experiences. How can we craft high-quality narratives about our lives, reframing pain and struggle as part of a journey of growth and evolution?

HEAL YOUR BODY

We often take superficial steps to maintain our bodies—exercise routines, diets, cosmetic efforts—but rarely do we focus on deep, inner healing. What does it mean to truly heal our bodies from the inside out?

HEAL YOUR INNER WOUNDS AND TRAUMAS

Every one of us has experienced trauma and carries inner wounds. It's a universal part of being human. Yet most people never fully acknowledge this pain, let alone do the work to heal it. This can lead us to become trapped in cycles of reactivity and suffering, impacting both ourselves and those around us. How can we heal our psychic wounds?

Without healing all three of these aspects of ourselves, we're not fully in charge of our lives. Ask yourself: *Who is driving my car?* If you're not consciously at the wheel, something else—an old wound, a buried trauma—is doing the steering, often taking you down roads you wouldn't choose.

Healing means reclaiming the driver's seat, choosing to create rather than react, and living from a place of clarity, joy, and purpose instead of being controlled by invisible scars. It's time to heal yourself, so you can become a source of healing in the world.

HEAL YOUR STORY

We get to choose the story we tell about ourselves. It may be one of victimhood, or we may position ourselves as a hero, or as a learner—someone who has grown through challenge. Healing begins when we transform the narrative of being a victim. That shift enables us to find deeper meaning and purpose in our experiences, seeing how they shaped us into wiser, more resilient versions of ourselves—and stronger, more grounded leaders.

HEALING LEADERS PRACTICE
Frame Your Story

In this exercise, you will explore how to heal your story by telling it three ways, each with a distinct perspective. Keep it brief; the exercise should take about thirty to sixty minutes.

Start by writing the story of your life as a victim.

Raj shares:

> *I spent my early childhood in a tiny village with no electricity or running water. I grew up in a harsh environment where my grandfather and uncles treated women and workers like slaves. My father was*

absent until I was seven; he never once picked me up or hugged me. When he came back into my life, I was afraid of him, and we never grew close. I survived, but life has hurt me in so many ways.

Next, write your story again, but this time, as a hero.

Raj shares:

Despite the challenges I faced—an absent father, frequent moves, abuse all around me, and a difficult education—I persevered. I transcended all of it to become a successful academic and cofounder of a global movement, Conscious Capitalism, that is impacting countless lives.

Finally, tell your story as a learner.

Raj shares:

Throughout my life, I encountered many setbacks and traumas—losing my job, being cut off from my family, navigating a challenging marriage, and raising a special needs son. But each of these experiences helped me grow, deepening my understanding of my life's purpose and shaping me into a more mature, empathetic, and loving human being.

While acknowledging both our wounds and our accomplishments is vital, there is unique power in viewing life through the lens of learning. As leaders, this perspective strengthens us, like an inoculation that fortifies resilience against future challenges. It fosters self-trust—the kind of trust that reassures you that no matter what life throws your way, you have the inner strength to face it.

Adds Nilima:

Looking back, I appeared to grow up in a "functional family"—a harmonious, patriarchal home where my father played the benign leader and my mother, my sister, and I willingly allowed him to take the lead. On the surface, it seemed ideal. Yet, like clockwork, every ten years brought a crisis that became a crucible for my personal growth.

At five, I watched my mother battle tuberculosis. At fifteen, I discovered she had breast cancer. At twenty-five, my father survived a near-fatal car accident that left him permanently disabled. At thirty-five, I learned that my husband had colon cancer—a moment that forever altered the fabric of our small family. orty-five signaled the beginning of the end of my marriage. And at fifty-five, I finally took charge of my own life, stepping into a new chapter as a single woman and Integral Yoga practitioner, devoted to my higher purpose: empowering women and sharing India's timeless wisdom with the world.

In hindsight, each of these harrowing crises—each long, dark night of the soul—was a turning point, forging me into the woman I am today. They shaped and refined me, stripping away illusions and awakening a more fully embodied version of myself. The life I live now is not in spite of those experiences, but because of them.

HEAL YOUR BODY

Most people ignore their bodies until it's too late. Many of us work in professions that center on the mind, with the body treated as little more than a vehicle for transporting our thoughts.

Years ago, while in Brazil, Raj thought he was having a heart attack. A medical check confirmed he was okay—but on the flight home, his heart rate suddenly spiked to 160 without warning. His life was stressful. He was relying on alcohol to cope, and he'd gained weight and felt exhausted. Though he exercised now and then, he'd never really prioritized his body's overall well-being.

In 2022, Raj and his partner Neha decided to make their health their top priority. Every December, they now spend three weeks at Sitaram Beach Retreat, an Ayurvedic healing center in Kerala, India. Each day, they wake at dawn, walk on the beach, practice yoga and meditation, and enjoy nourishing meals and restorative massages with herbal oils. This experience provides a profound physical, mental, and spiritual reset and revitalization.

Ayurveda, one of the world's oldest medical systems, originated in India nearly 4,000 years ago. The word comes from the Sanskrit *ayus* (life) and *veda* (knowledge), meaning "the science of life." It's a preventive, holistic approach that aims to restore balance through diet, lifestyle, herbs, meditation, and yoga. By maintaining internal harmony, Ayurveda helps manage stress, aids digestion, and boosts immunity.

Our bodies are incredibly wise—and extremely polite. At first, they whisper to us that something isn't right. Then they gently nudge. If we continue to ignore them, they eventually shout. Raj didn't want to wait for a full-blown crisis to learn his lesson, waking up in a hospital bed thinking, *I need to change my life*. He chose to listen and act earlier. What if we all did the same? What if we stopped using and abusing our bodies, and started partnering with them?

Think of yourself as the CEO of an exceptionally complex organization: your body, a masterpiece shaped by billions of years of evolution. Every part—your heart, lungs, kidneys, muscles, skin—is a stakeholder, relying on your conscious leadership. You have a responsibility to ensure the whole system thrives.

How can we partner with our bodies, rather than treating them as slaves to our desires? For years, Raj was at war with his lungs as a smoker (until he was 26), his liver with regular drinking, and his digestive system with an indulgent diet. The Ayurvedic retreat was as much an education as a healing experience, teaching us how miraculous our bodies are. It showed us that the body knows how to heal itself, if only we follow a few simple rules.

A foundational concept in Ayurveda is *Ama*, which means "not-me." *Ma* is you—your true self—while *A* negates it. Ama is anything in the body that doesn't belong and needs to be removed. Everything we consume and are exposed to becomes part of us, yet much of what we take in harms the body, which then struggles to eliminate these toxins. A core element of Ayurvedic healing is *Panchakarma*, a series of five cleansing processes that help restore the body's natural balance.

For most of human history, our greatest challenge was undernutrition. Today, in much of the world, the problem is overconsumption. The body becomes overloaded, forced to work overtime to clear out what it doesn't need. It's like overwatering a houseplant—the soil becomes waterlogged, and the roots begin to rot. In the same way, our systems become overwhelmed.

It's vital to treat the root cause of any illness, rather than focusing on individual symptoms. Imagine a beautiful city where the garbage collectors go on strike.[4] Trash begins to pile up in the streets, making the city unlivable. Rats appear, spreading disease across neighborhoods. It's tempting to say, "We have a rat problem, we need exterminators!" But the real issue isn't the rats, it's the garbage. If you don't get rid of the trash, the rats will keep coming, regardless of how many you eliminate.

How to Eat

Western (or allopathic) medicine has brought incredible advances, especially in emergency and surgical care. However, its approach tends to focus on symptoms and specialization, often isolating a problem and treating it without addressing the body's interconnected systems. Alleviating a symptom without resolving underlying imbalances may relieve suffering in the short term, but it can disrupt the body's intricate harmony over time.

Ayurveda offers a profound "owner's manual" for our bodies, including guidance on what—and how—to eat. Unlike the Western medical system, Ayurveda recognizes that each of us is unique, with different needs. This individuality is expressed through *doshas*, the fundamental energies that govern our physical and mental characteristics. There are three doshas—*Vata*, *Pitta*, and *Kapha*—each representing a blend of the five elements (earth, water, fire, air, and ether). Each of us has a unique combination of these doshas, with one or two typically dominant. This medley determines our constitution and our dietary and lifestyle needs. To maintain health, it's essential to keep the doshas in balance.

In Ayurveda, food is not merely fuel; it is a source of harmony for the body, mind, and spirit. Yet most of us rush through meals, often distracted by screens or multitasking. We treat eating as a chore to be completed quickly, often relying on unhealthy "fast food"—arguably one of the more harmful innovations of the modern world.

Ayurveda teaches us to eat the right food for our body type, in the right amount, at the right time, with full mindfulness. It encourages us to reflect on the journey our food has taken from the earth to our plate, considering the farmers who grew it, the earthworms, bees, and butterflies that contributed to its production, and the hands that cooked and served it. Eating in this way becomes a spiritual experience and a practice of deep gratitude.

Chewing is vital to digestion. Eating slowly allows 30 to 50 percent of carbohydrate digestion to occur in the mouth, aided by enzymes in saliva. This eases the load on the digestive system and supports better nutrient absorption, weight management, and overall gut health.

To eat mindfully, Ayurveda suggests:

- Eating meals at the same times each day: breakfast around 8:00 a.m., lunch around noon, and dinner by 6:30–7:00 p.m.
- Starting the day with a small amount of fruit, which digests differently from other foods, and waiting a while before eating anything else
- Eating only cooked, easy-to-digest foods for dinner
- Taking a leisurely walk after dinner, which aids digestion and promotes relaxation

The Awareness Prescription

As a hospitalist in the Kaiser Permanente system in California, Dr. Neha Sangwan cared for patients admitted to the emergency room with severe conditions like heart attacks and strokes. She often saw the same patients returning with similar issues, years after their initial visits. She realized that, while she was alleviating their symptoms, she wasn't truly healing them; she helped them through their crises but didn't address the root causes.

Eventually, practicing in this high-stress environment led her to burn out. During a medical leave, she recognized a deeper flaw in the way medicine was practiced. She became certified in functional medicine, diving into the connections between food, lifestyle, and health and learning that stress is a core factor in up to 90 percent of illnesses. This realization inspired her to develop what she calls the *Awareness Prescription*.

The night before one of her patients was to be discharged, she would say to them, "I hope to see you again—but not here. Maybe at the theater or the grocery store. If you're willing, answer these five questions by journaling tonight. If you do so, I will spend an extra thirty minutes with you tomorrow before you're discharged to get to the root of your health challenges and do what we can to make sure you don't come back here with the same issue."

The questions she asked were simple but profound, uncovering insights that standard treatment could not:

"WHY THIS?" In other words: Why do you think this happened to you? Why did this specific part of your body break down? What does this mean to you?

"WHY NOW?" Consider: Why did this happen at this moment in your life? Why not last year, or five years from now? What message was your body trying to deliver to you right now?

"WHAT SIGNALS MIGHT I HAVE MISSED?" Hindsight often brings clarity. Looking back, what early warning signs did you ignore? When was your body whispering, trying to get your attention?

"WHAT ELSE IN MY LIFE NEEDS TO BE HEALED?" Here, people would often break down, sharing painful truths: "I've carried trauma from serving in the Vietnam War for decades and never dealt with it," or "I haven't spoken to my mother in five years."

"IF I SPOKE FROM THE HEART, WHAT WOULD I SAY?" This question allowed patients to release the emotional pain they'd carried for years, pouring out words of sorrow, regret, or yearning. Responses were often unexpected: "I've felt deep sadness for so long."

Over time, Dr. Sangwan asked these questions of nearly 3,000 patients. The patterns she noticed in their replies eventually led her to write a book, *Talk Rx*, exploring how unhealed emotional pain and an inability to communicate with ourselves and others can manifest as physical illness.

The Awareness Prescription is a powerful tool—not only for medical crises but for any personal or professional challenge. It enables us to dig beneath surface symptoms and figure out what's really going on, so we can address the root cause rather than apply a temporary fix. It reminds us that true healing happens at the source, when we find the courage to face our lives with honesty.

Invest in Yourself

Self-care should not be treated as a luxury, or an act of selfishness—it's essential. The more you invest in your well-being, the more you are able to positively impact the world around you.

Dr. Vignesh Devraj, lead physician at Sitaram Ayurvedic Retreat, observes that when people list their life priorities, work and family almost always come first (in either order), followed by "having fun." Health is usually relegated to fourth place or lower, until advancing age or a health crisis suddenly catapults it to the top of the list—often too late.

But imagine what would happen if you put your health first from the beginning. Would that reduce your ability to excel in your work, care for your family, or enjoy life? Quite the opposite. When you prioritize your health, every aspect of life improves. You have greater resilience and presence, and more energy to give to your loved ones, your work, and your passions. You can wait for one of life's wake-up calls to make health a priority, or you can choose to start investing in it now and enjoy the lifelong dividends of vitality, joy, and clarity.

By putting our health and well-being at the forefront, we prepare ourselves to live, give, and love fully. Investing in yourself is an investment in your family, your work, and your purpose. It is an act not of indulgence but of generosity, one that affects everyone you touch.

HEAL YOUR INNER WOUNDS AND TRAUMAS

Healing also requires us to confront and address the psychological wounds we all carry, whether they stem from extraordinary circumstances or everyday hardships. Trauma can result from any overwhelming or deeply distressing experience that challenges a person's ability to cope, leaving lasting psychological scars. In the

United States alone, it is estimated that 12 to 15 million adults suffer from post-traumatic stress disorder (PTSD) each year. Lifetime prevalence rates reveal that nearly 7 percent of Americans, and 3.9 percent of the global population—some 320 million people—have experienced PTSD at some point in their lives.[5]

PTSD generally arises from extreme trauma, often manifesting in combat soldiers, first responders who have faced life-and-death situations, survivors of torture or abuse, and individuals who have experienced solitary confinement. However, virtually all of us carry what can be described as *post-traumatic stress injury* (PTSI)—an injury resulting from experiencing, witnessing, or hearing about potentially traumatic events.[6] The symptoms are similar and can be triggered by a broad range of events at any stage of life, from bereavement or painful breakups to financial strain, physical illness or injury, and the repeated micro-aggressions of daily life.

Many of us fail to recognize our traumas—especially those from childhood. Childhood experiences that can be traumatic, especially if not adequately supported or processed, include emotional neglect, parental conflict or dysfunction, bullying or peer rejection, separation or abandonment, academic or performance pressure, cultural or social marginalization, and economic hardship or instability.

Few among us are untouched by some degree of trauma, and its effects ripple through our emotions, behaviors, and relationships. Our unhealed traumas shape our lives in profound ways. They drive our reactions, fuel our fears, and build defense mechanisms we may not even realize exist. Trauma can keep us in a perpetual state of hyper-vigilance, mistrust, or numbness, influencing how we connect with others and navigate the world. The journey of healing isn't about erasing painful memories, but rather integrating them—finding ways to live with them, grow from them, and ultimately transcend them. In doing so, we gain hard-won wisdom that we can use to help others face and heal their own traumas.

Four Kinds of Trauma

Acknowledging that trauma is a shared human experience allows us to treat ourselves and others with greater compassion. Healing our internal wounds—whether deep and acute or subtle and long-standing—is essential to reclaiming our lives. It moves us beyond reactivity and empowers us to become the conscious authors of our own experience.

There are four primary forms of trauma that shape human life: personal, family, ancestral, and collective. Together, they influence our emotions, behaviors, and relationships in ways we may not always recognize.

Personal Trauma

Personal trauma is often the result of distressing events you have experienced directly—such as serious accidents or illnesses, sexual or physical abuse, or intense bullying. It can also arise from absence—the essential things you should have received but didn't. For example, every child needs love, emotional support, and nurturing physical contact from their caregivers. When such needs go unmet, it can leave lasting psychological scars. Both kinds of personal trauma—those caused by harmful presence and by harmful absence—can affect your sense of safety, self-worth, and worldview.

Raj shares:

> *My personal trauma centers on my relationship with my father. While living and teaching in Boston, I met a woman I wanted to marry—a choice that represented my own values and autonomy. When I informed my father, I encountered immediate and intense opposition. Despite his extensive education and global experience, he reacted forcefully to the idea of his son marrying someone outside of our Rajput culture. He immediately threatened to disown me.*
>
> *The conflict escalated into a traumatic struggle, with my father resorting to increasingly extreme measures to dissuade me. He threatened to curse our marriage, and even attempted self-harm to get me to change my mind. The most devastating incident came when he pointed a gun at me, declaring that he would rather not have a son than allow me to defy him in this way. This traumatic event was so painful that I erased the memory of it entirely (known as "dissociative amnesia") for thirty-three years, until a cousin told me what had happened.*

The rift between us continued for five painful years. When my son was born, my father refused to acknowledge him, deepening the wound. The trauma from these events was further compounded when our child began to show signs of special needs, which my wife attributed to my father's "curse." The scars from these years ran deep, affecting not only my relationship with my father but the legacy I carried into my own family.

Family Trauma

Family trauma refers to trauma embedded in your family of origin—the unresolved pain, challenges, or hardships that shaped your parents or caregivers. While you may not have experienced these events firsthand, you grew up in the shadow of their impact. For example, if a parent grew up in a war zone, in poverty, or in an abusive household, the psychological scars left by those experiences likely influenced their behavior and parenting style and, in turn, affected your sense of self and safety.

Raj shares:

My father spoke often of a "curse" that hung over our family, citing a history of suicides, violent or childhood deaths, and severe illnesses. The dark origin of this supposed curse came to light through my cousin, who revealed a hidden family atrocity that had been buried for generations. My grandparents had had thirteen children. Six did not survive infancy, and six grew into adults I had known for my whole life. The missing thirteenth child, I learned, was an aunt who, as a teenager, had been raped by a priest and become pregnant—a situation that our culture's rigid honor codes could not tolerate. To preserve the family's reputation, she was erased in a so-called "honor killing." From that day on, no one spoke of her; her memory was banished from the family history. Those two souls—my aunt and her unborn child—were never properly mourned, given no final rites or remembrance.

Many in my family believe this unacknowledged tragedy lay at the heart of the curse my father spoke of. The psychological weight of this trauma affected not only my generation but also our children.

Ancestral Trauma

Ancestral trauma goes a step further. Emerging research in epigenetics provides compelling evidence that the effects of trauma can be biologically "imprinted" and passed down through generations. Traumatic events experienced by our ancestors—such as slavery, genocide, displacement, or persecution—can subtly shape emotional and behavioral responses in later generations. For instance, some evidence suggests that African Americans, on average, exhibit a heightened fear of dogs. This fear is believed to trace back to the era of slavery, when dogs were weaponized to instill fear and maintain dominance.

Ancestral trauma is part of our genetic and emotional inheritance. Many of us have ancestors who were either victims or perpetrators of suffering—or both. These legacies can leave lasting, damaging imprints.

Raj shares:

> *My family's ancestral trauma stems from our history as defenders of India's rugged northwestern frontier, in the border state of Rajasthan. For centuries, our ancestors faced constant invasions, living in a perpetual state of readiness for battle. Many of them died in battle. The women and children, knowing they faced potential capture, enslavement, and abuse, sometimes chose* Jauhar*—mass suicide—rather than fall into the hands of the invaders.*
>
> *This legacy of violence, fear, and sacrifice runs deeply through my lineage, embedded within our very DNA. The trauma of lives lived on the edge of survival has likely left an imprint on me and my family today.*

Collective Trauma

Collective trauma refers to the large-scale wounds we experience together as a society or species. Climate change, for example, poses an existential threat that has left many—especially young people—grappling with "climate anxiety." The COVID-19 pandemic was a global trauma that fundamentally altered lives, economies, and social dynamics. Additionally, the rise of authoritarianism and social fragmentation in many parts of the world has led to growing fear, polarization, and a sense of instability, causing further collective trauma and affecting how we relate to one another.

Healing the Legacy

These layers of trauma are complex, intertwining across generations to form an inheritance of pain, resilience, and survival. True healing means not only freeing ourselves from the grip of the past but also reshaping the legacy we pass on. By breaking the cycles of silence, repression, and untreated wounds, we begin to write a new story. In this way, we offer our children—and ourselves—the possibility of a future marked not by fear or inherited pain, but by connection, strength, and healing.

Raj shares:

After learning the origins of the "curse" on my family, I traveled to India to initiate a healing ceremony, gathering the entire extended family to confront the crime of my aunt and her baby being killed in the name of the family's honor. I did this to end the conspiracy of silence that had shrouded her story for so long, give voice to her suffering, and acknowledge the wounds this event had inflicted on our family, rippling through generations.

For some family members, this history was either unknown or something they preferred to leave in the past. But I strongly believed it was essential for us to collectively honor my aunt's existence, to speak her name, to acknowledge her child, and to openly seek forgiveness—not just for our family's role in her tragic death, but also for the choice to conceal it.

Our ceremony of remembrance was not simply about reconciliation; it was about reflecting on our family's ancestral identity and purpose. We spoke together about our heritage as warriors—those traditionally charged with the protection and defense of others. This role of protector was the essence of our cultural lineage. Yet, as we acknowledged, somewhere along the way, that noble duty had been lost. Recent generations of our family had used their power and privilege in ways that harmed those they were meant to protect. The healing ceremony, in part, was an attempt to reclaim and recommit to our true dharma—our sacred duty—as protectors.

In honoring my aunt's memory and seeking forgiveness, we hoped to release the weight of shame and silence that had bound us, to bring healing not only to her spirit, but to the entire family. This experience revealed the profound importance of facing our painful histories as a step toward healing and rediscovering the shared higher purpose that runs through our lineage.

The ceremony was a powerful reminder that healing can only begin when we acknowledge the truth, however painful. In facing our shadows, we reclaim not just our history but also the strength and purpose that are our birthright, transforming cycles of suffering into paths of renewal and restoration.

Dealing with Trauma

To heal, we must first confront our trauma and say, "Yes, this happened. I can no longer ignore it. I cannot push it away. I must face this."

One of the most common—and destructive—ways people cope with trauma is by numbing it, often through drugs or alcohol. While these may offer temporary relief, the suffering inevitably returns. Others turn to high-risk activities, like extreme sports, for an adrenaline boost that helps them feel alive and briefly escape the pain. Though less harmful than substance abuse, this too is a form of avoidance. Any kind of escapism fails to address the wound itself, allowing the trauma to remain just beneath the surface, waiting to resurface.

Raj shares:

This is how my father dealt with his trauma. He carried the secret of the honor killing—the silenced tragedy that had marked our family for generations. Forbidden from speaking of it, he had no outlet, no support, and no way to process his pain. He numbed himself daily with alcohol, and then needed sleeping pills to rest at night. The only time I saw him smile and laugh was after a few drinks, when the mask of his pain momentarily lifted.

So what does a constructive path to healing look like? To deal with trauma, we must first *reveal* it and *feel* it; only then can we *heal* it, as depicted in Figure 13.

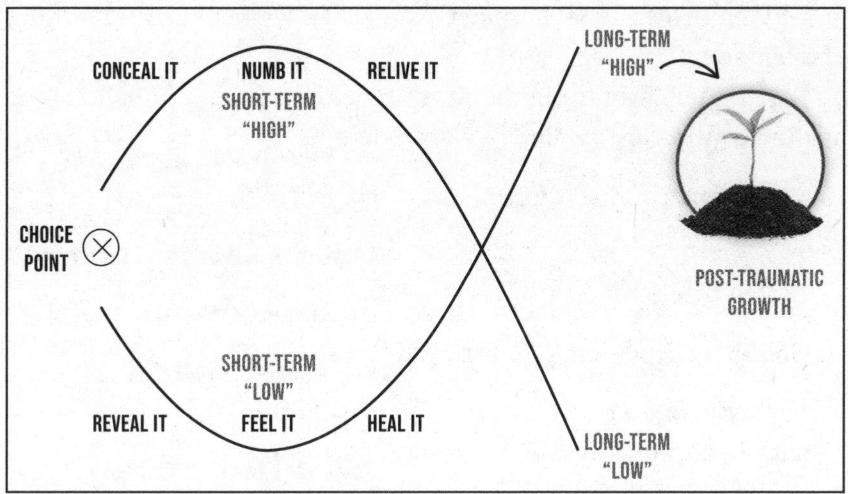

FIGURE 13. Dealing with Trauma. Adapted with permission from Neha Sangwan, MD.

The first step is to bring the trauma into the light—to talk about it openly, to break the silence. As children's television host Mr. Rogers once said, "If it's mentionable, it's manageable." By naming our trauma, we begin to dissolve its hidden power over us. Revealing it releases us from the secrecy and shame that allow it to fester.

After we've spoken our truth, we must allow ourselves to feel its full weight. This means granting ourselves permission to grieve, to cry, to revisit the pain we may have long buried. This can be an intensely emotional process, and it may lead to a temporary low as we reexperience the sorrow, fear, or anger of the original wound. But this is essential; we must move *through* the pain, not around it.

Healing doesn't happen overnight. Once we've revealed and felt our trauma, we can begin to work on it in different ways. The best results often come when trauma and addiction are addressed both physiologically and psychologically. There are practices that can help us process trauma from the body outward, such as somatic therapy, meditation, journaling, or simply creating space in our lives for self-care and nurturing. Healing might also involve reconnecting with trusted friends or loved ones, finding creative outlets, or seeking professional support. Every step we take is a reclaiming of our power.

Fortunately, we are living in a time when many modalities for healing trauma are available. These include:

- Acceptance and commitment therapy
- Biofeedback
- Cognitive processing therapy
- Eye movement desensitization and reprocessing (EMDR)
- Hypnotherapy
- Inner child work
- Internal family systems
- Neurofeedback
- Outdoor adventure therapy
- Prolonged exposure therapy
- Psychedelic-assisted psychotherapy
- Psychodynamic therapy
- Somatic therapy
- Trauma systems therapy
- Trauma-focused cognitive behavioral treatment

Healing is not an easy path, and it requires courage. But through this process of revealing, feeling, and healing, we open ourselves to a life that is no longer dictated by our past. Marshalling the courage to confront our deepest pain is also the key to our liberation.

Nilima adds:

> *In all my years of helping others heal and working on healing from my own journey's traumas, I have found that at the very bottom of all the unpeeling we do of the layers of pain lies unmet, unacknowledged, unprocessed grief. I often sum it up with the insight, "All healing lies on the other side of grieving." Paraphrasing our friend Quanita Roberson, a grief expert: "Grief is just love with nowhere to go."*
>
> *Once we find the courage and will to face our pain, unpacking it layer by layer, we find the unshed grief sitting at its center. Through therapy or self-awareness, we can and must process this grief, this sadness that has gotten stuck in our system and now threatens our physical and psycho-spiritual well-being. We must release that trapped love—for ourselves, or for someone else—to move on.*

The Gift of Post-Traumatic Growth

When you face your trauma fully and unflinchingly and work to heal it, an extraordinary gift awaits on the other side: *post-traumatic growth* (PTG). Emerging stronger not despite the trauma but because of it, you become more resilient and empowered than if you had never experienced the hardship at all. Sailing smoothly through life without challenges may seem desirable, but it rarely gives us the depth, empathy, and strength that come from working to overcome adversity.

Post-traumatic growth refers to the profound psychological shifts that can occur after wrestling with deeply challenging or traumatic experiences. Unlike resilience, which involves returning to a pre-trauma state, PTG is about transformation. It's the personal evolution that occurs when trauma becomes a catalyst for growth. People who experience PTG often report a renewed appreciation for life, a deepened sense of purpose, strengthened relationships, increased personal resilience, and a broader view of life's possibilities. Rather than merely surviving, PTG allows us to thrive.

Gabor Maté speaks of this as "the wisdom of trauma." Trauma, he suggests, is not just something that shapes our behaviors and worldview—it holds the potential for insight, healing, and transformation. When we, as individuals and communities, acknowledge trauma and actively work through it, we foster collective healing. By confronting our wounds with compassion, we reconnect with our authentic selves and gain wisdom that can guide us toward greater empathy, understanding, and wholeness.

The Japanese art of *Kintsugi* beautifully illustrates this concept. When a piece of pottery breaks, it is repaired with a mixture of gold dust and lacquer, turning the cracks into luminous seams. The repaired object is not only more beautiful but also stronger than before, as it has been fortified along its invisible fault lines—the places where it was weakest.

We all carry our own "precious scars"—evidence of wounds we've worked to heal and the resilience we've cultivated. These golden seams are not flaws to hide; they are marks of strength and transformation. They are badges of honor, reminding us of our capacity to grow through adversity and equipping us to help others deal with similar challenges. This is a powerful way to, as Viktor Frankl suggests, "find meaning in our suffering."

Reflect on your own life. Have you or your family of origin experienced traumas that remain unresolved? Consider the wounds that may live within you, passed down through generations. Reflect on the collective traumas—global unrest, natural disasters, or the recent pandemic—that may have impacted you psychologically. Acknowledging these layers of trauma is the first step in transforming pain into strength.

EMBRACE THE JOURNEY OF HEALING

Healing is not a one-time act; it is an ongoing journey—a commitment to revisiting and reintegrating the parts of yourself that feel broken or abandoned. In healing yourself, you take responsibility for your own well-being and, in doing so, free yourself to contribute more fully to the world. Healing releases us from reactive patterns, transforms pain into wisdom, and clears the way for joy, creativity, and love to flow through us.

Know that this work is not only for your own sake—it is a gift you offer to the world. Every wound you tend to, every insight you gain, becomes a source of strength not just for you but for those around you. Like a stone dropped into still water, your healing sends ripples outward, helping to restore a world also in need of repair.

As you reach the end of this journey, reflect on the path you've traveled through these seven steps. Each one has invited you to look deeply within, discover your true self, and nurture that self with intention and compassion. Consider the gifts you've received along the way. By knowing yourself, you've connected with the foundation of who you are. By loving yourself, you've shown yourself the compassion you may once have reserved only for others. By being yourself, you've brought authenticity into every part of your life. In choosing yourself, you've stepped out of victimhood and affirmed your worth. By expressing yourself, you've given voice to your deepest truths and allowed your unique gifts to shine through your purpose. By completing yourself, you've balanced the masculine and feminine, the elder and child within. And now, by healing yourself, you've woven all of these into a wholeness that allows you to flourish.

Take a moment to feel gratitude for the journey you've undertaken and to appreciate the courage it required. Let this be the beginning of a new chapter in your life, one where you apply what you've learned to continue growing, nurturing, and healing. Each day offers a fresh opportunity to deepen your relationship with yourself, to bring more compassion, presence, and joy into your life.

In healing yourself, you have opened the door to becoming a source of healing in the world. And that is a gift beyond measure—one that will continue to unfold, enriching and empowering you and those whose lives you touch in ways you may never have imagined.

CONSCIOUS LEADERS SPEAK
Heal Yourself

To heal yourself is not to erase pain, but to transmute it, to alchemize it into a source of wisdom, growth, and joy. For conscious leaders, this journey often begins in the heartbreak of grief, burnout, identity rupture, or historical reckoning. What emerges, in time, is leadership that is rooted not in unresolved wounds, but in conscious love.

Doug Rauch cautions us to distinguish between spiritual bypassing and true healing. "Healing yourself isn't the same as loving yourself. You can feel love without ever facing your pain. That's spiritual bypassing—using positivity to avoid the real inner work. True healing is about turning toward the wounds—not to wallow, but to bring them into the light. To feel them, name them, release them—so they stop steering your life from the shadows." There's a scene in the movie *Gandhi* that has stayed with Doug for decades. "A Hindu man, tormented by guilt after killing a Muslim child, says to Gandhi, 'I know I'm going to hell.' Gandhi replies, 'I know a way out. Find an orphaned Muslim boy. Raise him as your own—but raise him as a Muslim.' That's radical healing: turning your wound into love and wisdom."

Simon Cohen speaks of letting go of the whip. We often mistake self-cruelty for discipline. Healing requires tenderness. "We're so hard on ourselves. We push even when we're broken. We demand 110 percent—even in pain. But you can't run at full speed forever. Healing means saying, 'I'm enough.' It's giving yourself permission to rest, forgive, and let go. It means being tender with yourself. I used to blame myself for everything. Healing is softening that voice. If we don't forgive ourselves, we live with regret. And regret leads to darkness. Healing brings us back to light. In the end, that's where we're going—the endgame is love."

For Timothy Henry, healing is not a linear arc, but a spiral. The wound returns, but so does the light. "Healing isn't one and done. It's peeling an onion. You think you've done the work—then another layer comes up. For me, it's still that early wound—that crying child wondering, 'Why is nobody coming?' And healing means letting him in. Not pretending it didn't happen, but also not staying stuck. It's about moving through."

Kristin Engvig's healing has unfolded through ancestral repair, spiritual realignment, and communion with the natural world. "I've done so much ancestral healing—mother wound, cultural wound. It helped me find my light. Sometimes healing doesn't come through words. You send light. You hold presence. And something shifts." Kristin also sees the role of nature in healing. "I used to think freedom was about travel, voting, doing. Now I know real freedom is inner. It's choosing to rest, to trust, to be in rhythm with nature. These days, I meditate with trees. I rest in winter. I rise in spring. I no longer try to control the cycle. I am part of it."

Morad Fareed's path—shaped by intergenerational and political trauma—has revealed pain not just as burden, but akin to an organ in his body. "I'm Palestinian. Just existing feels like resistance. There's family trauma, political trauma. For a long time, I numbed it. Healing began when I stopped hiding. I let the pain in. I held multiple truths at once. I could feel grief and still lead. Still love. Suffering, I've come to believe, is evolutionary. It's the growth of new perception organs. We are still becoming. The human system is not complete."

For Gervase Warner, healing has meant grieving what didn't go the way he had hoped, while staying open-hearted. "Healing has been iterative. I've done the deep work—the Landmark Forum, coaching, spiritual exploration. But how my time at Massy ended is still raw. I've written about it. I've processed it. But the mood lingers. Maybe healing isn't about closure. Maybe it's about continuing to care—even when the ending wasn't what you wanted." Gervase has also started to confront the reality of his heritage as a man with African roots. "There's collective healing too. In confronting the legacy of slavery in the Caribbean, I saw how I'd internalized and reproduced systems I meant to dismantle. That broke me open. Healing has to be personal and historical. Otherwise we keep recreating what we haven't reconciled."

John Mackey finds healing not in analysis, but in divine remembrance. "Healing doesn't come from outside. It comes when we open to divine guidance. For me, A Course in Miracles is that voice. It reminds me: I'm already whole. I just forget sometimes. Every time I return to that stillness, I remember who I am—eternal, loving, whole. That's what healing is to me. Not fixing. Remembering."

Ed Freeman offers a nuanced take—healing not as cure, but as integration and self-awareness. "I've always had a hard time with the word 'healing.' It implies something's broken. I see life as hard, but not pathological. I've been shaped by Freud—where the point isn't to 'get over it,' but to understand why you are the way you are. When I was sixteen, I took sleeping pills out of my mother's hand. That was traumatic. But I didn't bury that memory; I've worked with it. That's part of knowing myself—not healing, necessarily, but living with awareness."

Marisa Lazo's practice, shaped by meditation and Buddhist teachings, emphasizes equanimity rather than escape. "Healing isn't about fixing everything. It's about embracing the fact that life is hard—and beautiful. You heal one wound, and another comes. It's a lifelong dance. The Buddhists taught me: Suffering is part of life. If we resist it, we suffer more. If we accept it, we grow."

For Avivah Wittenberg-Cox, healing happens through story—through writing her truth, and then offering it back to the world. "I've always healed through writing. That's how I processed my divorce. I write to understand—and then to share." Interestingly, Avivah sees aging, too, as a kind of healing. "I've never been happier than in my sixties. And I want younger women to know: It gets better. We heal the collective story by telling a new one."

Across these voices, we find a shared truth: Healing is not about erasing what hurt us. It's about transforming it, composting it so that it can nurture our evolving self. Feeling it. Learning from it. Offering it back to the world as wisdom, compassion, or creative expression. Whether through meditation, story, ritual, or remembrance, these leaders have faced what they once fled—and emerged more whole, more human, and more equipped to help others do the same.

CHAPTER 9

An Upward Spiral of Growth and Love

We are not going in circles, we are going upwards.
The path is a spiral; we have already climbed many steps.
—HERMANN HESSE

The journey you have embarked on in this book is not one of linear progression, but of conscious evolution. Your life will grow more joyful, and your leadership more impactful, as you deepen in self-awareness, love, humility, and spiritual integration. There is no upper limit to that process. As John Mackey put it in our interview: "The inner universe is infinite. Just like the cosmos, there's no limit to who we are. The more we learn, the more we realize how much more there is to discover. I'm still healing, still learning, still becoming. And that's the real adventure."

SEE THE STEPS AS INTERWOVEN AND INTERPENETRATING

Betty Sue Flowers offers us another way to think about the journey: Rather than steps on a path, think of the seven stages in this journey as *doorways*. Any of them can lead to all the others. Whichever one you enter can become a portal to wholeness and healing:

> *These steps are not rungs on a ladder. They aren't linear. In fact, they're not really steps at all. They're more like doorways—or chapels in a great cathedral—each one a sacred space you can enter at any time. You may enter through whichever one is open to you in the moment. One day you might walk through Be Your Self, another day through Know Your Self. Once inside, all others become accessible, since they all connect. You don't graduate from one to the next—you move among them. You circulate. These aren't stages of development—they're portals into presence. Each one is a way of returning to the deeper self.*
>
> *Some days, you may not be able to love yourself. But maybe you can choose yourself, or begin to heal yourself. And from the space you enter through that doorway, love may eventually arise. That's the beauty of this model—it's forgiving, spacious, alive.*
>
> *You could make a daily practice of it—drawing one step like a card from a sacred deck. "Today, I draw Choose Your Self. That's my practice." Tomorrow, it might be Complete Your Self. That, too, is a form of choosing—choosing to be present, choosing to trust synchronicity, choosing to live in a world that is not random but full of grace.*
>
> *You might even make it a ritual. Light a candle. Sit in stillness. Ask, "Which part of myself needs tending today?" Then choose—not from the mind, but from the heart. That's a practice of profound listening, of honoring your own unfolding.*

THE HEALING POWER OF NOW

The miracle of the present moment is that it holds extraordinary potential for healing (Figure 14). In this moment, we can begin to heal the past. We can create and sustain the conditions for a healthy future. We can heal our relationships with our parents, children, colleagues, or partners—even if those people are no longer with us. The present is a time to release old stories, embrace new perspectives, and build deeper, more meaningful connections.

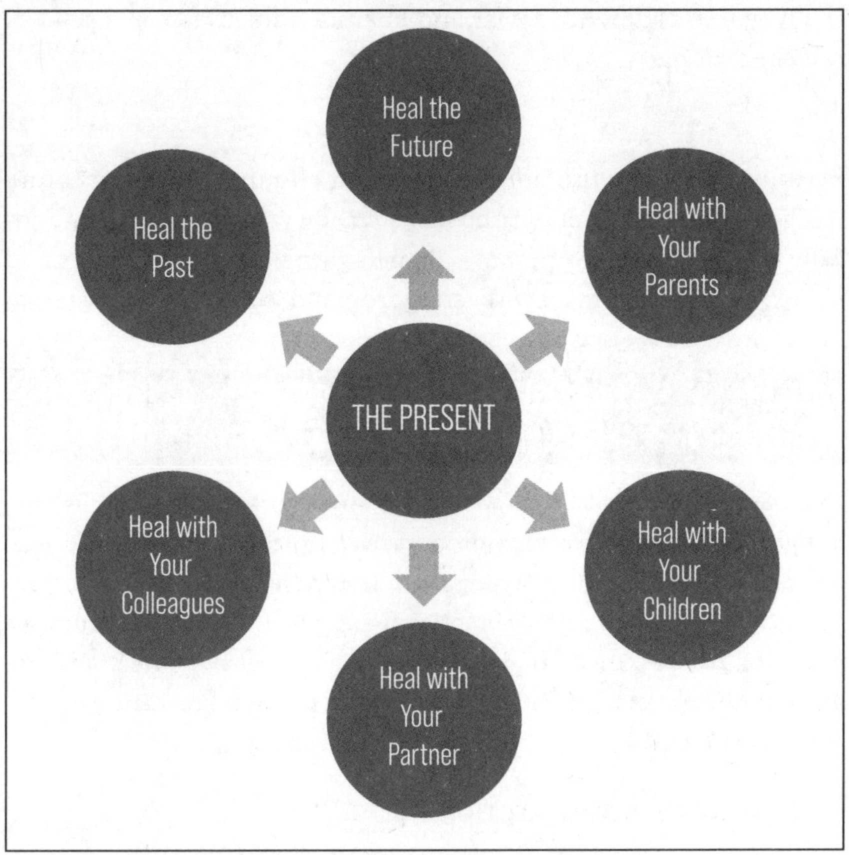

FIGURE 14. The Healing Power of Now

Heal the Past

The present moment offers a powerful opportunity to change the way we view our lived experiences. While we cannot change the events of the past, we can transform our relationship to them. For instance, we might carry pain stemming from traumatic experiences and failures. In the present, we can acknowledge those feelings and choose to release them or to extend forgiveness. This shift invites compassion for both ourselves and others, as we recognize that the actions of everyone involved were affected by their own limitations and struggles. Healing the past in the present moment is a way to reclaim our power and liberate ourselves from cycles of hurt and blame.

Heal the Future

By fully inhabiting the present, we lay the foundation for a future free from the weight of past burdens. When we approach life mindfully, we make choices that are aligned with our deepest needs and values, rather than merely reacting from old, conditioned patterns.

HEALING LEADERS PRACTICE
Become a Self-Cleaning Oven

Neha Sangwan teaches that we should strive to become "self-cleaning ovens," continuously working on ourselves to learn from life and heal wounds early, rather than letting them fester and grow.[1] When we consistently process and release emotional and psychological "buildup," we prevent it from accumulating and distorting our behavior, relationships, and self-perception. This ongoing inner work promotes resilience, adaptability, and mental clarity. To become a self-cleaning oven:

COMMIT TO SELF-REFLECTION

Engage in regular self-reflection, analyzing your reactions, emotions, and behaviors. This allows you to gain insight into your motivations and recognize how past wounds might be influencing your present. Practices like mindfulness and journaling support this by helping you observe your thoughts without judgment.

CONTINUALLY PROCESS YOUR EMOTIONS

Emotions are natural responses to life's events. But if left unprocessed, they can solidify into reactive patterns, limiting beliefs, or even chronic physical pain. By practicing "emotional hygiene"—acknowledging, understanding, and working through emotions as they arise—you can prevent them from becoming long-term emotional baggage that inhibits well-being. This may involve therapy, expressive activities such as art or movement, or practicing gratitude to reframe painful experiences.

EMBRACE GROWTH AS A LIFELONG JOURNEY

View life as an ongoing process of learning and healing. Rather than seeing pain and difficulty as setbacks, treat them as opportunities for growth—stepping stones rather than roadblocks. Psychologist Carol Dweck calls this a "growth mindset": a willingness to learn from experiences, adjust behaviors, and integrate new insights.[2] With this perspective, you can meet life's challenges with greater resilience.

DEVELOP HEALTHY BOUNDARIES AND PRACTICE SELF-CARE

Just as regular cleaning helps an oven function well, self-care and boundaries maintain your emotional well-being. Practice self-care by setting aside time for rest, relaxation, and activities that bring joy, allowing you to recharge and stay connected with your authentic self. Healthy boundaries help prevent external stressors from penetrating too deeply, keeping your internal environment clean and manageable.

LEARN AND LET GO

Work actively to let go of past hurts and grievances. This might involve forgiving others (or yourself) for past mistakes, accepting things that cannot be changed, and returning your focus to the present moment. When you confront and learn from painful experiences, you reduce the likelihood of bitterness or resentment building up over time. This helps clear space for new insights and greater peace.

This approach to life cultivates a healthy, proactive relationship with yourself—one that transforms pain into wisdom and clarity into personal growth. It's a mindset that leads to resilience and contentment, empowering you to navigate life with grace and integrity.

Heal with Your Parents

Healing in the present moment also allows us to tend to wounds inflicted by our parents or other caregivers, even when the scars run deep. This healing can occur whether they are still with us or not. By revisiting painful memories with fresh awareness, we can process our emotions and begin to understand the humanity in them—their strengths and flaws, and the limits of their own healing. This process frees us from cycles of resentment and opens pathways to forgiveness, acceptance, empathy, and compassion (Figure 15).

When a child doesn't receive the nurturing, unconditional love they need from a caregiver, it can leave profound psychological wounds that shape their psyche, leading to destructive thoughts and behaviors such as people-pleasing, risk avoidance, and self-doubt.

Psychological literature refers to these as "mother wounds" and "father wounds." As Raj described earlier in the book, he carried a deep father wound for much of his life. He and his father eventually "reconciled" after five painful years of estrangement over Raj's choice of who he would marry, but it would take another twenty-five years to achieve genuine healing. Raj cycled through waves of anger and bitterness until, one day, he watched the film *Tuesdays with Morrie.* Morrie's most powerful lesson was, "If I could live life again, I would forgive everyone for everything. All the bitterness I

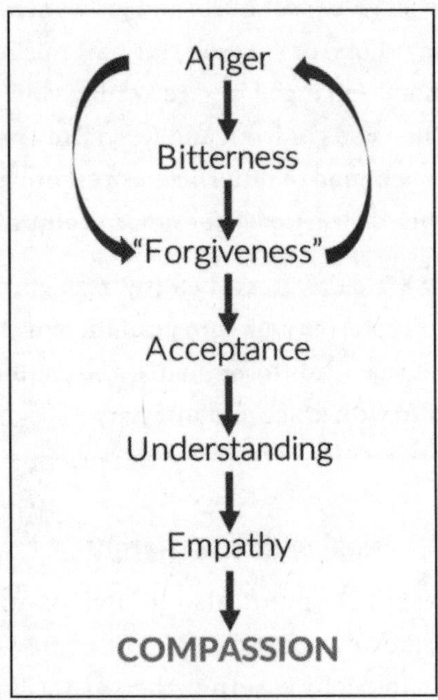

FIGURE 15. The Path to Healing

have carried around only poisoned me. It hasn't helped me in any way." Upon hearing those words, Raj resolved to forgive his father for everything. But true forgiveness is complicated: How do you forgive someone who has never apologized?

A few months later, an Art of Living course taught Raj five simple but impactful principles, one of which was the importance of accepting people as they are. Accepting others' flaws and differences helps create stronger bonds and reduces unnecessary conflicts that arise from unmet expectations. People act as they do for reasons we may never fully understand, and acceptance means allowing them to be as they are. Raj asked the instructor, "Is acceptance the same as forgiveness?" He responded, "No. Forgiveness implies you're right and they're wrong. Acceptance simply sees them as they are."

Raj shares:

From that moment, I committed to accepting my father as he was. Over time, as I observed him and reflected on his life, understanding began to replace resentment. I recognized how powerfully cultural expectations and traditions had shaped him. He was deeply influenced by his upbringing. Marriage in India often carries expectations beyond personal happiness. As one of the rare highly educated people from our warrior class, my marriage was expected to enhance our family's social standing.

Understanding grew into empathy as I considered his history. My father, too, had faced his father's harsh demands. He had dreamed of becoming a doctor, but my grandfather refused to allow him to attend college. When he finally relented, he insisted my father study agriculture to benefit the family's large ancestral farm. My father yielded, abandoning his dream. Later, when he fell in love with someone else, my grandfather swiftly arranged his marriage to my mother. Again, my father gave in. When he built a promising career in North America, my grandfather accused him of abandoning the family. Reluctantly, my father returned to India, sacrificing his career and dreams.

Absorbing these stories, I moved from empathy to compassion. This shift was healing; I began to see him without the triggers of old wounds. One day, he told me bluntly, "I love your brother more than I love you." Instead of feeling hurt, I understood. He had been able to be a father to my brother from infancy, forming a bond he couldn't have with me or my sister.

Heal with Your Children

In addition to healing with our parents, those of us with children may also need to heal with our children. We can begin to break cycles of pain by being present with them, listening deeply, and choosing love over reaction. The present moment gives us the opportunity to respond differently than we might have experienced ourselves, laying the foundation for a healthier relationship. In doing so, we halt the transmission of unresolved pain and offer our children the gift of growing up in an environment shaped by understanding, acceptance, and compassion.

Most of us were never formally taught how to parent. All we have are the imperfect models our own parents provided. When we become parents, we are in some ways still children ourselves, trying our make our way in a challenging world. We carry unhealed wounds and unintegrated shadows within us, and despite our best intentions, we may unknowingly pass that pain on to our children, falling short of offering them the unconditional love and attunement they need.

But once we recognize and accept the reality that we are all wounded, and that we are all capable of healing, we can choose a new way forward. A valuable resource for this is the *Hello Again* workshop (and forthcoming book) created by Gabor Maté and his son Daniel.[3] With the tagline "A fresh start for parents and their adult children," the workshop provides tools to transform strained parent–adult child relationships by clearing away entrenched emotional patterns and making way for authentic connection. It explores the complex ways early family dynamics can carry into adulthood, creating tension or misunderstanding, and advocates examining the origins of these dynamics to prevent repeating past conflicts. The aim is to help participants move beyond inherited roles and expectations and instead relate to each other as independent adults with unique experiences and needs.

Key lessons include developing compassion for the impacts of childhood wounds, letting go of past grievances, and cultivating mutual curiosity. Gabor and Daniel Maté emphasize that healing doesn't come from "fixing" or advising but from presence and understanding. Parents are invited to recognize that their adult children seek connection, not correction, and adult children are invited to allow space for their parents to grow and show up differently. Drawing on their own experiences, with vulnerability and humor, the Matés model a path to a renewed relationship rooted in the present, rather than the past.

For Nilima, this is the final ongoing piece in her healing journey as a mother. Using the "victim to hero to learner" framework (page 149) she writes:

> *Leaving a thirty-four-year marriage—one that often made us appear to the world as the "golden couple with the golden family"—created unexpected frictions in my relationships with both my son and my daughter.*
>
> *If I were to narrate this from a place of woundedness, I might say that for many years I felt unseen and unheard for who I truly was. As my work in the world grew—especially after the launch of* Shakti Leadership *in 2016—I sensed that not only was my success unacknowledged or celebrated, it was, at some level, resented. Perhaps there was a subconscious fear: What might this growing success mean for the family unit we had always prioritized above all else? Would it threaten to break us apart?*
>
> *If I were to tell my motherhood story as the heroine of my own journey, I would say I persisted despite the odds—and despite rarely, and often grudgingly, being supported by my children. As they became more "Westernized" in their thinking, I felt them drift further away from me. They did not share my spiritual path, my love of ancient wisdom, or my deep devotion to India—a devotion that now fuels my calling to serve the country through my work.*
>
> *Each of them was grappling with their own frustrations and challenges, pursuing meaningful but difficult paths in renewable energy and cultural entrepreneurship—fields not easily supported in India's current economic or political climate. Their political views also began to diverge from mine, sometimes leading to judgments I had to absorb. And yet, I chose to keep the channels of communication open, doing my best to reach out, connect, or hold space with unconditional love—even while often crossing lines and slipping, because of my own blind spots.*

They understandably had not anticipated the emergence of a "new mom"—a woman stepping fully into her third act, her "Q3," with her own voice, aspirations, and destiny. They seemed to want just "Mom," not a full-blooded woman with a calling. But I refused to let my need to be a "good mother" stand in the way of fulfilling my purpose.

Ultimately, this led to the heartbreak of separation. My deepest and most sacred longing had always been to walk the path of purpose with my husband, to grow together in service. Letting go of that dream nearly destroyed me. But I came to accept that our paths had diverged. And now that we had completed the hands-on parenting phase—what Indian tradition calls Grihasthashram*—it was time for me to enter* Vanaprastha: *the turn to the forest, the withdrawal from daily domestic duties to tend to life's larger garden.*

As much as I longed to be the perfect mother—and to be understood by my adult children—I had not anticipated the trauma they would experience when I left their father. Perhaps, in their minds, the family no longer represented the "safe home" they could return to, to be nurtured and cherished as they always had been. I sensed that I may have became, in their eyes, the "villain" who fractured the family by selfishly choosing "me" over "us."

As I continue to process the heartbreak of feeling that my mothering may not have been "enough," and reflect on how much of my life force I gave to my husband's healing, I find solace in becoming a learner in my own parenting story.

My deep interest in Jungian psychology and the alchemical path of individuation has helped me reframe what has happened. I now see my family of four as a compound made of distinct elements—each one needing to be separated, purified, and transmuted to its higher essence before they can be reunited into a truer, more golden form. In alchemy, this is the path to wholeness. But the process must begin with the "sacrifice" of one element to trigger the transformation. Perhaps, in our case, I was that element.

Each of us—my son, my daughter, my husband, and I—is markedly different. Maybe we must each embark on our own heroic journeys, confront our inner demons, and heal our individual wounds before we can come back together in a higher harmony.

I had a vivid dream in 2004 that now feels prophetic. We were all on a train, heading to the ocean on a family holiday. Somehow, we got separated. Yet we found each other again soon after—and the reunion was filled with joy and relief. Each of us exclaimed, "I stayed on the train—I thought you got off!"

As I seek to heal and learn from my relationships with my son and daughter, I move gently through the emotional landmines—of hurt, judgment, and, above all, unexpressed love that longs to burst forth.

Some days are good, others less so. But overall, I choose to trust that this painful unraveling is part of a deeper healing—that we are each, in our own way, walking each other home, to a place where we can be more fully ourselves, and more joyfully together.

Heal with Your Partner

Healing in the context of a marriage or significant partnership is profound work—so rich and complex a topic that it could easily fill an entire book. (In fact, many such books already exist; two we highly recommend are *How to Be an Adult in Relationships: The Five Keys to Mindful Loving* by David Richo, and *Partnering: A New Kind of Relationship* by Hal and Sidra Stone.)

Chapter 7 is our most focused offering on this theme. To recap: When each partner takes responsibility for becoming whole—integrating their ego and shadow, reconciling their inner masculine and feminine (anima and animus), and aligning their personal self with their higher self—they create the conditions for a healed and healing relationship.

This kind of inner work requires immense willingness and openness. It is often hard, triggering, and not always reciprocated by the other. We see many relationships break under this strain, and more people choosing to remain single. Women tend to burn out due to not feeling emotionally met, while men often carry unprocessed trauma from having had to suppress their feminine and spiritual sides to survive in a patriarchal system.

Indeed, patriarchy has wounded us all—women, men, and those beyond the binary.

If the institution of marriage or long-term partnership is to survive and evolve, it must be grounded in a new paradigm: individuals who heal themselves into wholeness and offer that healed self as a gift to the relationship.

The story of alchemy described by Nilima in the previous section serves as an archetypal metaphor for what couples and families are being called to undergo—a transformational process that purifies and elevates each individual so that, together, they can cocreate structures of love, harmony, care, respect, and mutual growth.

To do this, we must consciously cultivate and apply key capacities—love, acceptance, forgiveness, letting go, and the courage to say no—in the right balance, toward ourselves, our partners, and the situations we encounter.

When approached with awareness and intention, intimate partnership can become a powerful path to personal wholeness. This is perhaps the most challenging path we will ever walk, yet it is also the one that holds the greatest promise: to lead us back to the very source of love itself. Whether we ultimately stay together or choose to part, the journey can still be sacred, healing, and whole, helping us reunite all the parts of our owned and disowned selves.

Heal with Your Colleagues

Just as our relatives form a system at home, our colleagues form a system at work—a collective that must remain in dynamic equilibrium. For such a system to thrive, there must be a healthy and reciprocal flow of energy, communication, and respect among all its members.

The most powerful tool we offer for addressing challenges in the workplace is the Dharma Triangle, introduced in Chapter 5.

To reiterate: We invite you to reframe your workplace "villain" as a challenger—someone who shows up to help you grow, raise your game, and reclaim your voice and power. This might mean standing firm and not accepting the unacceptable. Or, in some cases, it may mean exiting the situation gracefully and wisely, creating space for new opportunities for everyone involved.

Building the capacity for this kind of conscious engagement requires learning proven tools of communication and conflict transformation. We strongly recommend Nonviolent Communication (NVC), which teaches empathy-based dialogue and foundational negotiation skills that can turn tension into trust.

We also highly recommend practicing the *Four Agreements* from Don Miguel Ruiz's classic book of the same name:

- Be impeccable with your word.
- Don't take anything personally.
- Don't make assumptions.
- Always do your best.

Nilima adds:

I like to think of work as a Yoga of Collaboration. In fact, I've begun drafting a playbook for it—rules of engagement that help us not only work well together but also grow as individuals. My vision is to integrate the best of ancient wisdom and modern management into a framework that all team members agree to live by. When we do this, our organizations transform from places we need therapy to recover from to sacred grounds where we are free to become the best versions of ourselves—flourishing in leadership and in life. As John Mackey once famously said, "Whole Foods is my ashram. . . . It is where I do my deepest spiritual work."

The foundational rule of the playbook is based on the 51/49 principle: Each person agrees to spend 51 percent of their time and effort on growing their own consciousness, only then dedicating the remaining 49 percent to helping others heal and grow. Without maintaining this balance, we risk getting burned out, or doing harm while wishing to do good.

RAJ'S YEAR OF CONSCIOUS AWAKENING

In 2018, Raj turned sixty—a big milestone for most humans. Few of us ever feel the age we are; inside ourselves, we're all the ages we ever were. But reaching sixty seems different; it marks the end of the second act and the beginning of the third and final act of our lives. It is a time for taking stock, for making sense of things, for sharing lessons learned.

In those days, Raj lived with an almost panicked sense of urgency. Before one book was published, he would already be agonizing about the next one. He was deeply engrossed in his next book project at the time, *The Healing Organization*. Then, within weeks of each other, four women who had each made a big difference in his life said the same thing. It was some version of this: "You're writing a book about healing. *What about your own healing?* You can't write a book about healing if you don't heal yourself first."

Raj jokingly responded, "I don't have time for that; I have a deadline!" But then, he had the wisdom to listen to these sage voices. He asked the book's publisher for a five-month extension and accepted invitations for a number of healing and growth experiences that he had previously declined.

Synchronistically, Nilima had long planned a "Shakti Tour," a spiritual journey in June 2018 to Ladakh, high in the Himalayas on the border between India and Tibet. Raj recalls, "We crossed mountain passes at an elevation of 22,000 feet, as we made our way from one valley to another, soaking in the deep Buddhist wisdom that is rooted in that part of the world. I learned a lot about healing and suffering and life in general. I had my sixtieth birthday there."

Next came a silent retreat at Peace Village in New York State, where Raj spent four days in the company of thirty-five other seekers. Walking around in nature with his journal and spending time in blissful silence, he received numerous downloads, including the seven steps that are the core of this book.

That summer also included a trip to the Amazon rainforest, organized by Lynne Twist and the Pachamama Alliance. This was a profound ten-day experience of deep immersion in nature and the wisdom of the shamans, including an ayahuasca journey that revealed more to Raj about healing than he could have gleaned from years of therapy or research.

Raj also started working with a coach, Suzanne, for the first time. When she asked him to tell her the story of his life, he told her about the culture he came from, his troubled relationship with his father, and how his professional life had turned around when he wrote the book *Firms of Endearment*, which led to the launch of the Conscious Capitalism movement and everything else that followed.

Suzanne sat silently with her eyes closed for a minute, then said, "Do you realize that you spent the first forty-five years of your life trying to impress your father? That was never going to work. Now, you've spent the last fifteen years honoring your mother with your work. Everything you've done since—writing *Firms of Endearment*, launching the Conscious Capitalism movement, and all the books you have written since—is bringing your mother's loving energy into the world of business. That's what's missing there: healthy, loving mother energy. You are more like your mother than you are like your father. It was your destiny to be the channel for that to come to the world of business and capitalism."

It took a minute for Raj to absorb this insight, which was completely new to him. He replied, "Wow, I never thought of it like that. I think you're right."

Then Suzanne asked, "Does your mother know that? You need to call her and tell her." Raj hesitated, saying, "We don't talk like that in my family." Suzanne insisted, "It's important. You need to have this conversation."

Raj then suggested that he would speak to his mother in person when he travelled to India a few weeks later. Suzanne replied, "Your mom is eighty-one years old. You don't know what will happen in three weeks. You need to call her." Raj said, "Okay, I'll call her."

Raj recalls:

> *The next morning, I called her. I said, "Mummy, I want to tell you something I've never said to you before. I want you to know that everything that I've done in my life that has made any difference in the world is because of you. It's what you taught us and how you lived your life and how you loved us. That's what the world needs. The world has plenty of what Papa stands for." She started crying and said "Raj, I am nothing. I am nothing." By this time, I was in tears too. I said, "No, Mummy, you are everything. Without your love, I don't know if still I'd be alive. I don't know if my life would mean anything at all."*

Too many of us take our mothers for granted. I had always loved her deeply, but I had never said those things to her before. I was grateful that I got to express my deep love and appreciation for her. It became the most healing conversation of my life, and was deeply meaningful for her as well.

LAST WORDS

Both of Raj's parents passed away suddenly in 2019, within four months of each other. In a matter of months, he went from having two parents to none.

Raj shares:

Like Gandhi, my mother's life had been her message: "Never cause unnecessary pain in anyone's heart." She reminded us of this often and embodied it fully, living and loving by this principle every day. By the time I reached India, she was already unconscious in the hospital, so I did not get a chance to speak with her one last time. A few weeks after she passed, I did a plant journey back in the United States to connect with her. In my visions that night, she came to me as her truest self—regal, powerful, and beautiful. It reminded me of the end of a Broadway play, when the actors return to the stage as themselves, no longer bound by their roles. She had lovingly and dutifully played her roles all her life—daughter, sister, wife, mother, aunt, grandmother, great-grandmother. Now she was liberated to be her authentic self, freed of those identities.

She spoke to me as clearly as if she were in the room with me: "Raj, remember never to cause pain in anyone's heart. I know that is your nature. And know that you will always be loved." I quietly sobbed through the night, feeling the deep pain of her absence and overwhelming gratitude for having been mothered by her.

Though I did not have the opportunity for a final conversation with my mother, I was, fortunately, able to speak with my father. I was in India for a wedding. He was already in the hospital when I arrived, looking shockingly frail. A few days later, he came home, and I thought, "This might be the last time I see him." I didn't want him to leave this life with any heaviness, guilt, or regret over what had happened between us. If I could, I wanted to release him from that weight.

I sat by his bed, held his hand, and said, "Papa, I want to thank you for giving us such an interesting life, filled with so many unique experiences. You worked very hard for us. I love you, and I thank you." He looked at me with a half-smile and said, "Raj, you are your own boss."

I responded, "Well, that's a good thing, right?" I've always felt that no one should have a "boss"; the very word has long troubled me. It derives from the Dutch word baas, *meaning "master," in the context of slavery. No human being deserves to be "bossed"—we need guides, leaders, and fellow team members instead.*

My father just smiled, saying nothing more. Perhaps he meant, "You never listened to me and selfishly did your own thing." But I choose to interpret it as a moment of grudging respect. He hadn't been able to live his life on his terms, constrained by his own father's strictures. But I had defied convention, and had been willing to pay a price to live by my own compass. I hadn't conformed to the roles expected of me—as an Indian, a man, a Rajput, a marketing professor, or an academic. I crafted my own way and did my best to stay true to it, even when it was hard, even when it meant not fitting in or defying tradition.

I believe my father's last words carry a message for all of us: Each of us should be our own boss. Better yet, we should be our own best friends and coaches. Nobody should boss you around—not even yourself.

Grief or Relief? Choose Your Legacy

Two funerals in four months. The contrast between them struck Raj deeply. His father's passing was solemn and significant. He had been a commanding patriarch, impacting countless lives in ways good and bad, large and small. He was a larger-than-life figure, charismatic and powerful.

The occasion reminded Raj of his grandfather's death years earlier—an even more weighty event because it meant the division of ancestral land and titles in a feudal culture. His grandfather had been a harsh, unloving, and controlling figure. When he died, there was a palpable sense of relief. Raj's uncles and cousins had been waiting anxiously for him to pass so they could finally have the freedom to live their own lives.

At Raj's father's funeral, he couldn't help but notice no one was crying except his mother. He felt sad and wanted to weep, but he couldn't summon any tears. His sister and brother didn't cry either.

Raj remembers:

> *Four months later, when my mother died, no one could stop crying. I was in tears in Boston when I learned she was hospitalized and declining. On my way to India, I called my brother from the Frankfurt airport. He said, "We told her you're coming, and she seems to be doing better." I broke down in the airport lounge and again on the long flight to Delhi. When I arrived at her bedside in the hospital, she was comatose and unresponsive. I cried as I held her hand, and kissed her forehead as she lay there, harnessed to a tangle of wires and tubes. When she passed a few days later, our grief was overwhelming. Everyone was sobbing. A week later, when family members gathered to talk about her, the tears just kept flowing, along with a deep sense of gratitude that she had been a part of our lives.*
>
> *A question echoed in my mind: "What will happen when I die? Will there be grief or relief?" This felt like a profound life lesson.*
>
> *When my father died, there was a degree of relief and little grief. He had tremendous brilliance, charisma, and personal power. However, he did not come from love. His love, if it can be called that, was largely conditional: He loved you as long as you did what he wanted you to do.*
>
> *My mother's love was constant and unconditional; there was nothing I could have done to lose it. Yet she did not stand in her power—she stood by helplessly as my father caused great suffering for the family.*
>
> *For me, the holy grail is to strive to manifest both the power and impact that my father had and the deep, unconditional love that defined my mother. If I can get close to that, I will consider this a successful life.*

Think about the inevitable day of your own passing. Will people feel grateful that you were in their lives? Or will they feel indifferent? Many people live and die without leaving a trace, while others leave a lasting, positive legacy. Can we commit to living in such a way that people grieve deeply when we die and are filled with gratitude that we were here?

THE SHADOW SIDE: LIVING WITHOUT THE SEVEN STEPS

Before we close, let's explore a sobering thought experiment. What if we chose to live in direct opposition to each of the seven steps? What would such a life look like—and why do so many people unconsciously choose this path?

THE UNKNOWN SELF

Imagine navigating life as a complete stranger to yourself. You never discover what makes you unique, what values truly matter to you, or what your essential nature demands. You remain a mystery to yourself throughout your entire existence, never understanding why you react as you do or why your best intentions consistently fall short.

Your identity becomes a patchwork of others' expectations—family scripts, cultural programming, societal norms. This constructed self might function for years, even decades, but eventually the foundation crumbles. You find yourself profoundly unhappy, unfulfilled, and disconnected from others. Your life ends without you leaving a trace of authentic impact behind, because you never knew who you truly were.

THE UNLOVED SELF

Consider your life if you were one of the many people who navigate life not just without self-love, but often with active self-loathing. You neglect your physical health, abuse your body, and refuse to invest in your growth. This creates a vicious downward spiral—the less you love yourself, the less lovable you become to yourself, perpetuating endless cycles of self-neglect, abuse, and isolation.

THE MASKED SELF

Picture a life lived entirely behind masks, shape-shifting to meet others' expectations. Your mantra becomes "go along to get along." You master the art of people-pleasing, sacrificing authenticity for acceptance. Unable to feel your emotions—or express them when you do—you bury them deep inside, where they fester and eventually explode as rage or manifest as chronic physical pain or disease.

THE VICTIM SELF

What if you spent your entire life rejecting everything life gave you? You'd become a professional victim, constantly lamenting, "Why me?" You'd feel simultaneously entitled and perpetually disappointed, taking for granted every blessing while obsessing over what's missing.

Wise people treat the past as destiny and the future as free will. You do the opposite—raging against an unchangeable past while passively accepting a future you could actively shape. You become an expert at finding someone to blame (including yourself) for everything "bad" that happens, while remaining completely passive about creating anything good.

THE UNEXPRESSED SELF

Imagine never expressing your true self. You play it safe, always choose comfort over growth, and live reactively rather than purposefully. Driven by triggers and habits, not conscious choice, you drift through life with no purpose beyond earning a living and feeding your desires.

You live by "grab and go" instead of "give and grow," never risking vulnerability, never attempting anything that might reveal your true capacity. You live your entire life as a caterpillar, forsaking the creature of light, beauty, and contribution that you could have become.

THE INCOMPLETE SELF

Consider allowing yourself to be completely defined by your birth gender and current age. You live as a fraction of a human being, trapped by narrow definitions of who you're supposed to be. Because you never integrate your complementary qualities, you end up with the shadow aspects of each—hypermasculine domination or hyperfeminine submission, youthful recklessness or aged rigidity.

THE WOUNDED SELF

Finally, imagine refusing to acknowledge the wounds and traumas you've accumulated. You walk through life as a collection of unhealed injuries, unconscious of your triggers. You're not driving your own life; your wounds are. Not only do you suffer enormously, you inflict that suffering on others—especially those you claim to love and try to lead.

Your being becomes suffused with fear, anger, and suspicion. You never experience genuine peace or joy, relying on escapism for fleeting moments of relief. Your death is mourned by few.

Sadly, this shadow path isn't a caricature—it's the default setting for many people. Without conscious effort to know, love, be, choose, express, complete, and heal ourselves, we unconsciously drift toward these patterns.

The seven steps aren't just suggestions for improvement—they're essential practices for avoiding a life of quiet desperation. They're the difference between existing and truly living, surviving and thriving, leading from wounds and leading from wisdom.

The choice is always yours. The question is: Which path will you choose?

THE INFINITE SPIRAL OF GROWTH

We shall not cease from exploration
And the end of all our exploring
Will be to arrive where we started
And know the place for the first time.

—T.S. ELIOT

As we conclude this journey through the seven steps to recovery of self, you might feel that you've reached the end. But in truth, you're standing at the threshold of a new cycle of growth. Personal healing and growth are not linear paths with clear endpoints—they are spirals of continuous evolution. With each cycle through these seven steps, we emerge as more fully realized and perfected versions of ourselves, becoming ever more attuned to our deepest essence and more capable of expressing that essence in ways that uplift others.

Think of these seven steps as points on an upward spiral. When you complete the seventh step, you don't return to where you began; you arrive at a higher level of understanding, ready to *know yourself* once more.

Consider how different you are now from when you first opened this book. Perhaps you've released old beliefs, embraced new perspectives, or uncovered hidden strengths. The person completing this journey is not the same as the one who began it. And that is exactly as it should be.

When you return to *knowing yourself* after *healing yourself*, you'll do so with deeper wisdom, greater compassion, and renewed curiosity. The questions you ask yourself will have changed. The answers you find will reveal new layers of understanding. Your capacity for self-love will have expanded, your authenticity will have deepened, and your choices will emerge from a place of increased awareness.

This is the beauty of the spiral: Each rotation builds upon the last, integrating experiences, insights, and growth into an ever-expanding awareness of who you are—as a leader and as a human being. The challenges you face may seem familiar, but you'll approach them with new tools, greater insight, and heightened resilience.

Remember, healing is not a single event but a lifelong practice, a commitment to yourself and to others. Our hope is that this book inspires you to embrace each step with humility, joy, and the knowledge that as you evolve, you illuminate the path for others. Each cycle reveals new truths and invites you to reenter with fresh insights, an open heart, and a renewed sense of purpose.

As you continue to cycle through these seven steps, each iteration will bring unique gifts, challenges, and opportunities for growth.

Some cycles may focus on certain steps more than others. Some may move swiftly, while others require patient, careful attention.

With every loop through these stages, we grow; our understanding deepens, and our perspective broadens. This is what it means to be a healing leader: to possess the courage to meet oneself anew, to embrace change, and to share an ever-deepening wisdom with the world.

Trust this process. Trust that each time you spiral upward, you're not merely repeating; you're evolving—expanding your capacity to lead with authenticity, to heal with intention, and to serve with purpose.

As you close this book, know that this is not an ending—it is a new beginning, starting from a higher level of awareness. The journey continues. The spiral ascends. And you, dear reader, are always growing, always learning, always healing.

Take a moment now to honor how far you've come. Then, with gentle curiosity and renewed purpose, ask yourself: *Who am I becoming?*

Remember: this life of yours is not a static thing. It is an upward spiral of never-ending possibility, shaped by love, choice, and courage.

The next spiral awaits.

NOTES

CHAPTER 3

1 In the original tradition, metta is sent to all the people in your life who are suffering—not just your friends, but also your "enemies." It is understood that each of us is a manifestation of the universal self, and thus they are just another you.

2 Research has demonstrated that compassion-based meditation practices can lead to changes in brain function and structure and that metta practice increases positive emotions and reduces stress, which in turn can lead to improved social connections and overall well-being (including improved immune function and mental health). See Richard J. Davidson and Antoine Lutz, "Buddha's Brain: Neuroplasticity and Meditation," *IEEE Signal Processing Magazine* 25, no. 1 (2008): 171–174, *https://doi.org/10.1109/MSP.2008.4431873*; Barbara L. Fredrickson et al., "Open Hearts Build Lives: Positive Emotions, Induced through Loving-Kindness Meditation, Build Consequential Personal Resources," *Journal of Personality and Social Psychology* 95, no. 5 (2008): 1045–1062, *https://doi.org/10.1037/a0013262*; and Stefan G. Hoffman, Paul Grossman, and Devon E. Hinton, "Loving-Kindness and Compassion Meditation: Potential for Psychological Interventions," *Clinical Psychology Review* 31, no. 7 (2011): 1126–1132, *https://doi.org/10.1016/j.cpr.2011.07.003*.

3 Chris Gardner, "How I'm Living Now: Glenn Close," *The Hollywood Reporter*, April 8, 2020, *https://www.hollywoodreporter.com/news/general-news/how-im-living-now-glenn-close-1288088/*.

4 Nitin Shah, "The Powerful Emotional Empowerment Technique (EET)," *Institute of Clinical Hypnosis and Related Sciences blog*, April 15, 2015, *https://instituteofclinicalhypnosis.com/hypnosis/emotional-empowerment-technique/*.

CHAPTER 4

1 David Steindl-Rast, "5 Steps to Finding Your Vocation," VISION Vocation Network, 2015, *https://www.vocationnetwork.org/en/articles/show/434*.

2 The School of Life, "The Dangers of the Good Child," March 15, 2017, *https://www.theschooloflife.com/article/the-dangers-of-the-good-child/*.

3 Gay Hendricks, *The Big Leap: Conquer Your Hidden Fear and Take Life to the Next Level* (HarperOne, 2009).

4 Maslow's hierarchy of needs is a motivational theory in psychology that outlines basic human needs, often depicted as a pyramid. According to the theory, lower-level needs must be satisfied before higher-level needs can be addressed. From the bottom up, these are: physiological needs, safety needs, love and belonging, esteem, and self-actualization. See Saul McLeod, "Maslow's Hierarchy of Needs," *Simply Psychology*, March 14, 2025, *https://www.simplypsychology.org/maslow.html*.

CHAPTER 5

1 Thich Nhat Hanh, *No Mud, No Lotus: The Art of Transforming Suffering* (Parallax Press, 2014).

2 Javed Akhtar, in *Angry Young Men*, directed by Namrata Rao (Amazon Prime Video, 2024).

3 Stephen B. Karpman, *A Game Free Life: The Definitive Book on the Drama Triangle and the Compassion Triangle by the Originator and Author* (Drama Triangle Productions, 2014).

4 David Emerald, *The Power of TED: The Empowerment Dynamic*, 3rd ed. (Polaris Publishing, 2015).

5 By Sunil Savara; enhanced by Raj Sisodia. Used with permission.

6 When we do this practice in a workshop, we place a small flower in the hand of each participant at this point in the experience. When they open their eyes, most are moved to tears.

7 Joseph Campbell, *The Hero with a Thousand Faces* (Princeton University Press, 1949).

8 Christopher Vogler, *The Writer's Journey: Mythic Structure for Writers*, 3rd ed. (Michael Wiese Productions, 2007).

CHAPTER 6

1 Quoted in Polly Labarre, "Do You Have the Will to Lead?" *Fast Company*, February 29, 2000, *https://www.fastcompany.com/38853/do-you-have-will-lead*.

2 This practice is drawn from the work of Roberto Assagioli and his concept of *psychosynthesis*, which teaches that we each have an ego self and a higher self.

CHAPTER 7

1 Robert Kagan, *Of Paradise and Power: America and Europe in the New World Order* (Alfred A. Knopf, 2003), 3.
2 Joanna Barsh, Susie Cranston, and Rebecca A. Craske, "Centered Leadership: How Talented Women Thrive," *McKinsey Quarterly*, September 1, 2008, *https://www.mckinsey.com/featured-insights/leadership/centered-leadership-how-talented-women-thrive.*
3 Barry Johnson, *Polarity Management: Identifying and Managing Unsolvable Problems* (HRD Press, 2014).

CHAPTER 8

1 World Bank Group, "Measuring Poverty," accessed July 5, 2025, *https://www.worldbank.org/en/topic/measuringpoverty.*
2 Mark É. Czeisler et al., "Mental Health, Substance Use, and Suicidal Ideation during the COVID-19 Pandemic—United States, June 24–30, 2020," *Morbidity and Mortality Weekly Report (MMWR)* 69 (2020): 1049–1057, *http://dx.doi.org/10.15585/mmwr.mm6932a1.*
3 University of Hawaii at Manoa, "Strong Evidence Shows Sixth Mass Extinction of Global Biodiversity in Progress," *ScienceDaily*, January 13, 2022, *https://www.sciencedaily.com/releases/2022/01/220113194911.htm.*
4 This analogy is used by Dr. Vignesh Devraj, the head physician at Sitaram Ayurvedic Retreat. Used with permission.
5 National Institute of Mental Health, "Post-Traumatic Stress Disorder (PTSD)," accessed July 5, 2025, *https://www.nimh.nih.gov/health/statistics/post-traumatic-stress-disorder-ptsd*, and World Health Organization, "Post-Traumatic Stress Disorder," May 27, 2024, *https://www.who.int/news-room/fact-sheets/detail/post-traumatic-stress-disorder.*
6 D'Amore Mental Health, "What's the Difference between PTSD and PTSI?" June 21, 2022, *https://damorementalhealth.com/difference-between-ptsd-and-ptsi/.*

CHAPTER 9

1 Neha Sangwan, "What a Messy Space Reveals about Relationships, Part 1," Intuitive Intelligence, March 10, 2016, *https://intuitiveintelligenceinc.com/tag/self-cleaning-oven/.*
2 Carol Dweck, *Mindset: The New Psychology of Success* (Random House, 2006).
3 Hello Again Project, "Hello Again: A Fresh Start for Parents and Their Adult Children," accessed July 5, 2025, *https://www.helloagainproject.com.*

RECOMMENDED READING

In our effort to offer readers a complete journey, we have served as horizontal "beams" covering many vertical "columns" of specialization. We have included only the essence of each body of work included in this synthesis. We urge you to go directly to the source of any specific body of work or reference that may call you. We particularly recommend the following books:

Barletta, Marti. *Prime Time Women: How to Win the Hearts, Minds, and Business of Boomer Big Spenders*. Kaplan Publishing, 2007.

Barsh, Joanna, and Susie Cranston. *How Remarkable Women Lead: The Breakthrough Model for Work and Life*. Crown Business, 2009.

Beebe, John, ed. *Terror, Violence, and the Impulse to Destroy: Perspectives from Analytical Psychology*. Daimon Verlag, 2003.

Campbell, Joseph. *Goddesses: Mysteries of the Feminine Divine*. New World Library, 2013.

Campbell, Joseph. *The Hero with a Thousand Faces*. New World Library, 2008.

Estés, Clarissa Pinkola. *Women Who Run with the Wolves: Myths and Stories of the Wild Woman Archetype*. Ballantine Books, 1992.

Farrell, Warren. *The Myth of Male Power: Why Men are the Disposable Sex*. Berkley Publishing Group, 1993.

Gerzema, John, and Michael D'Antonio. *The Athena Doctrine: How Women (and the Men Who Think Like Them) Will Rule the Future*. Jossey-Bass, 2013.

Jaworski, Joseph. *Synchronicity: The Inner Path of Leadership*, 2nd ed. Berrett-Koehler, 2011.

Johnson, Barry. *Polarity Management: Identifying and Managing Unsolvable Problems*. HRD Press, 1996.

Kempton, Sally. *Awakening Shakti: The Transformative Power of the Goddesses of Yoga*. Sounds True, 2013.

Mackey, John, and Raj Sisodia. *Conscious Capitalism: Liberating the Heroic Spirit of Business*. Harvard Business Review Press, 2013.

Murdock, Maureen. *The Heroine's Journey*. Shambhala, 1990.

Rosin, Hannah. *The End of Men: And the Rise of Women*. Riverhead Books, 2012.

Sandberg, Sheryl. *Lean In: Women, Work, and the Will to Lead*. Knopf, 2013.

Sanford, John. *Invisible Partners: How the Male and Female in Each of Us Affects Our Relationships*. Paulist Press, 1979.

Sinek, Simon. *Leaders Eat Last: Why Some Teams Pull Together and Others Don't*. Portfolio, 2014.

Stone, Sidra. *The Shadow King: The Invisible Force That Holds Women Back*. Nataraj Publishing, 1997.

ACKNOWLEDGMENTS

Since we met at the Conscious Capitalism India conference in Mumbai in 2010, Nilima has been a constant source of deep wisdom, personal growth, and practical guidance in my life. Our collaboration for *Shakti Leadership* was a profound learning experience for me. Nilima helped shape my memoir, *Awaken: The Path to Purpose, Inner Peace, and Healing*, in important ways. I owe her my deepest gratitude and appreciation.

This book would not exist were it not for a serendipitous conversation I had with Nilima when we were coteaching a women's leadership program in Puerto Vallarta, Mexico. I asked Nilima to help me think through how to design a program I had been invited to lead at Tecnológico de Monterrey (where I am a professor of conscious enterprise), with the prompt "Who do you need to *be* in order to teach conscious business?" We had covered the "knowing" and "doing" aspects of conscious business with our faculty; now it was time to address the "being" aspect. When she saw the seven steps, she immediately lit up, seeing them as somehow divinely ordained. We codesigned a three-day immersive workshop around them. This book emerged from that workshop.

Nilima and I had such a delightful experience with Neal Maillet and Berrett-Koehler while working on *Shakti Leadership* that we did not hesitate in offering this book to them. I thank Neal for his enthusiastic advocacy for the book, his deep reading of it, and his expert editorial guidance. We are also grateful to the rest of the BK team for bringing this book into the world with such care and craft. We are especially grateful to Rachel Wheeler for her outstanding copyediting and to Ashley Ingram for designing a beautiful cover.

I would also like to thank the following people for making this book possible:

The organizers of the 2018 Call of the Times silent retreat at Peace Village in New York, led by Peter Senge, David Cooperrider, and Rita Cleary. This is where I received the seven steps as a direct download into my consciousness.

My partner, Neha Sangwan, who has been a loving source of growth and healing for me in the seven years we have been together. She has enabled me to see things that would otherwise be invisible to me and has influenced my thinking on each of the seven steps in important ways.

The conscious leaders we interviewed for the book, who shared their journeys in authentic and vulnerable ways, adding greatly to the wisdom it has to offer. They are listed here in alphabetical order: Avivah Wittenberg-Cox, Betty Sue Flowers, Doug Rauch, Ed Freeman, Gervase Warner, John Mackey, Joseph Jaworski, Kip Tindell, Kristin Engvig, Marisa Lazo, Morad Fareed, Simon Cohen, and Timothy Henry.

My Tecnológico de Monterrey colleague, Luis Gerardo González López, for helping to conceive of and launch the Healing Leaders workshop. He participated in the workshop alongside other faculty and several colleagues from the Conscious Enterprise Center: Francisco Javier Fernández González, Gabriel Renero Mariscal, María Martha Licón Sáenz, and Christiane Andrea Molina.

The faculty and administrators at Tecnológico de Monterrey, for their support for Conscious Capitalism and for the elevation of consciousness among the faculty and the many executives who have been though our programs. These include Jose Antonio Fernandez, Juan Pablo Murra Lascurain, and Ignacio De la Vega García.

Finally, I would like to acknowledge the impact that two Spiritual teachers have had on me: Sri Sri Ravi Shankar of the Art of Living Foundation and Sadhguru Jaggi Vasudev of the Isha

Foundation. These living masters are spreading loving universal wisdom and deep healing around the world in profound ways.

—Raj Sisodia
Boston, July 13, 2025

If I were to acknowledge only Raj Sisodia for the pleasure and honor of coauthoring this book, that alone would truly suffice. Of course, I must also express deep gratitude to our editor, Neal Maillet, and to Berrett-Koehler for so quickly saying "yes!" to our book proposal. These two have been game-changing and life-changing partners in my work in the world. It all began twelve years ago, when they said "yes" to help birth *Shakti Leadership*.

Much of what I bring to this second book—crafted with this dream team of Raj and Berrett-Koehler—arises from the body of work that continues to inform the Shakti Leadership mission, which I have since built and nurtured. That mission, in turn, is deeply inspired by and grounded in the Integral Yoga of Sri Aurobindo and The Mother, who serve as my ultimate reference point for any roadmap to elevate humanity and evolve the planet.

The Shakti Leadership model itself emerged from the convergence of Integral Yoga principles and the Conscious Capitalism movement, seeking to create a simple, step-by-step approach to Conscious Leadership (one of the four tenets of Conscious Capitalism).

What began as a personal synthesis to guide my own journey of awakening, wholeness, and self-leadership over the past twenty-eight years is now offered in support of leaders who may not have the time it requires to put things together themselves. It is the "elixir" I bring back from my own heroic journey, offered in service of all who are ready to lead from their deepest truth and highest self.

This work includes the most potent and catalytic elements drawn from leadership frameworks, transformational practices, and teachings from around the world. We are keenly aware that we stand on the shoulders of giants—authors, clinicians, researchers, scholars, facilitators, healers, leaders, and teachers—whose work has inspired and enabled this synthesis.

I wish to especially acknowledge the following key bodies of work:

- Joseph Campbell and Maureen Murdock's insights on myth and the hero/heroine's journey
- The foundational contributions of Sigmund Freud and Carl Jung to archetypal and depth psychology, particularly the "four-fold self" model as developed by Brian Skea
- The Integral Yoga of Sri Aurobindo and The Mother, along with their Shakti teachings
- The "deep dive model" of Conscious Leadership, developed by some of India's leading facilitators within the consciousness collaborative known as Chittasangha
- The Gateways to Presence, based on the Enneagram work of Don Riso and Russ Hudson
- The Drama Triangle by Stephen Karpman, and its conscious applications developed by David Emerald and the Hendricks Institute
- Polarity Thinking by Barry Johnson
- The Conscious Capitalism model developed by Raj Sisodia and John Mackey

My own contribution is a set of final insights and integrative builds that have helped shape a self-leadership model—one that can truly enable gender reconciliation, leverage diversity and inclusion, and evolve the workplace as well as the life space. I hope you, too, will be able to apply these steps in your own way, embodying that simplicity which lies on the far side of complexity.

Finally, I would like to acknowledge the Divine in Life itself. In all its sweetness and suffering, highs and horrors, goodness and grief, I keep the faith and hold it all as holy. My deepest gratitude to all these sources of wisdom.

May this book serve many.

—Nilima Bhat
Pondicherry, July 10, 2025

INDEX

Q

R

S

ABOUT THE AUTHORS

RAJ SISODIA is a founding member of the Conscious Capitalism movement, FEMSA Distinguished University Professor of Conscious Enterprise, and chairman of the Conscious Enterprise Center at Tecnológico de Monterrey. He is the cofounder and chairman emeritus of Conscious Capitalism Inc. and president of Awaken Inc.

Previously, Raj was FW Olin Distinguished Professor of Global Business and Whole Foods Market Research Scholar in Conscious Capitalism at Babson College. He also spent fifteen years at Bentley University as Trustee Professor of Marketing and Information Technology, department chair, and founder/director of the Center for Marketing Technology.

Raj was born in India and spent parts of his childhood in Barbados, California, and Canada. He was educated as an electrical engineer at the Birla Institute of Technology and Science (BITS, Pilani). He received an MBA in marketing from the Jamnalal Bajaj Institute of Management Studies in Mumbai, after which he earned a PhD in marketing and business policy from Columbia University.

Raj is coauthor of the *New York Times* bestseller *Conscious Capitalism: Liberating the Heroic Spirit of Business* and *Wall Street Journal* bestseller *Everybody Matters*. In 2003, he was cited as one of fifty leading marketing thinkers and named to the Guru Gallery by the Chartered Institute of Marketing. Bentley University honored him with the Award for Excellence in Scholarship in 2007 and the Innovation in Teaching Award in 2008. He was named one of "Ten Outstanding Trailblazers of 2010" by Good Business International and one of the "Top 100 Thought Leaders in Trustworthy Business Behavior" by Trust Across America for 2010 and 2011. In 2013 and

2015, Raj was named to the Thinkers50 list of business and management thinkers from India. He received an honorary doctorate from Johnson & Wales University in 2016 and the Business Luminary Award from Halcyon in 2021.

Raj has consulted with and taught executive programs for numerous companies, including AT&T, DPDHL, IBM, Kraft Foods, LG, McDonald's, Nokia, POSCO, Rabobank, Siemens, Southern California Edison, Sprint, Tata, Verizon, Volvo, Walmart, and Whole Foods Market. Since 2007, he has spoken over a thousand times on Conscious Capitalism and related topics to audiences around the world, including at the White House and the Vatican. He cohosts the podcast *The Conscious Capitalists* with Timothy Henry.

Raj has published sixteen books, including *Firms of Endearment: How World-Class Companies Profit from Passion and Purpose*, which was named a top business book of 2007 by Amazon.com. His most recent books are *Awaken: The Journey to Purpose, Inner Peace, and Healing*, *The Healing Organization: Awakening the Conscience of Business to Help Save the World*, and *The Global Rule of Three: Competing with Conscious Strategy*.

Raj has served on the board of directors of The Container Store and Mastek Ltd. He is a trustee of Conscious Capitalism Inc. and serves on the advisory board of several organizations, including the Fowler Center for Business as an Agent of World Benefit and PayActiv.

Learn more at *rajsisodia.com*.

NILIMA BHAT is a visionary, speaker, author, and coach in the fields of personal mastery, leadership, gender equality, and well-being. She served as a Distinguished Professor in Gender and Conscious Leadership in the Faculty of Excellence at Tecnológico de Monterrey and is known for her original thinking and facilitation of personal and systemic transformation.

Her extensive and pioneering work is captured in her two influential books: *Shakti Leadership: Embracing Feminine and Masculine Power in Business* and *My Cancer Is Me: The Journey from Illness to Wholeness*. Together, these works offer holistic and integrated approaches to leadership and resilience, charting new pathways toward a world that works for all.

An active supporter of Conscious Capitalism and Women's International Networking (WIN), Nilima also serves on the advisory boards of 20-first, MixR, and Peace Through Commerce. In 2022, she was awarded an honorary PhD by Jharkhand Rai University, in recognition of her "iconic and outstanding contribution in the field of women empowerment." Shakti Leadership also received recognition as a Home for Humanity in 2023.

At a time when the world seeks new models, her Shakti Leadership framework has been referenced in multilateral organizations and forums including the Nobel Peace Prize Forum, the United Nations, the World Bank, and the International Monetary Fund (IMF).

Nilima is currently focused on the following transformative initiatives:

- Building the Shakti Fellowship, in collaboration with the University of San Diego, WIN, and Skolkovo FLOW, with the mission of creating 100,000 women changemakers by 2030
- Leading the Truth and Reconciliation movement, dedicated to healing collective trauma and fostering inclusive peace on a planetary scale
- Organizing the Shakti Kumbh, the first-ever Kumbh Mela for spiritual traditions of the Divine Feminine, for which she received the INDICA Cultural-Changemaker Fellowship Award

Previously, Nilima led Corporate Communications for ITC Hotels, Philips, and ESPN STAR Sports before cofounding Roots & Wings, a leadership consultancy, in 2004. She has delivered leadership training and facilitation for organizations including Etsy, Genpact, Microsoft, Société Générale, Tata, Vodafone, Whole Foods Market, and YPO, as well as for academic institutions and developmental organizations such as Babson College, SKS Microfinance, and the University of San Diego.

An expert in Indian wisdom and wellness traditions, Nilima is a certified Sivananda teacher and practitioner of the Integral Yoga of Sri Aurobindo and The Mother. She is also a trained dancer and cofounded the dance company Sri Shakti to demystify Indic art and wisdom for international audiences. In partnership with the Centre for Behavioral Health at Hong Kong University, she developed and practiced the Integrative Medicine Model, *Sampurnah* (meaning "wholeness"), to help patients heal from cancer and other lifestyle diseases.

She lives in Pondicherry, India, serving as Global Goodwill Ambassador and Director - Special Projects for World Union, a spiritual organization promoting human unity based on Sri Aurobindo's philosophy.

Learn more at *shaktileadership.com.*

Also by Nilima and Raj

Shakti Leadership

Embracing Feminine and Masculine Power in Business

Too many people, men and women alike, have bought into a notion of leadership that exclusively emphasizes traditionally "masculine" qualities: hierarchical, militaristic, win-at-all-costs. The result has been corruption, environmental degradation, social breakdown, stress, depression, and a host of other serious problems. Nilima Bhat and Raj Sisodia show us a more balanced way, an archetype of leadership that is generative, cooperative, creative, inclusive, and empathetic. While these are traditionally regarded as "feminine" qualities, we all have them. In the Indian yogic tradition they're symbolized by Shakti, the source that powers all life.

Berrett-Koehler
PUBLISHERS

Berrett-Koehler PUBLISHERS

Dear Reader,

Welcome to the Berrett-Koehler Community—a global network of changemakers creating positive impact in their lives, organizations, and communities.

Our Mission: Connecting People and Ideas to Create a World That Works for All

We believe transformation is possible. While outdated paradigms of self-interest, exclusion, and hierarchy continue to hold back our communities and organizations, we know that change can happen. That's why we connect people with actionable ideas from leading experts who are already creating the solutions we need.

The BK Way

We're an independent publisher that practices what we publish. Our books, digital resources, and community offerings provide practical pathways for building more just, equitable, and sustainable organizations and lives. Whether you're transforming your workplace, community, or personal practices, our publications meet you where you are with tools that work.

But we don't just talk about positive change—we live it. Through "The BK Way," we put stewardship and purpose before profit. As a benefit corporation, we're legally committed to benefiting all our stakeholders: authors, readers, employees, communities, and the environment.

As our gift to you, claim your free bestselling ebook at bkconnection .com/welcome. You'll also receive fresh leadership insights delivered to your inbox from bkconnection.com/blogs/the-bk-exchange.

You Make the Difference

We're grateful to our readers, authors, and community members, who bring our mission to life every day. Your stories of transformation inspire us and show others what's possible.

Share how BK publications are making a difference in your world at bkconnection.com/impact.

Your friends at Berrett-Koehler

Join the Berrett-Koehler Community

Are you passionate about supporting independent publishing and reading diverse voices and perspectives? Join the BK Community Membership Program and become a part of a vibrant literary community. To support mission-based publishing while saving up to 30 percent on all books and attending exclusive events, visit ideas.bkconnection.com/bkcommunity-join to learn more and become a member.